UNIVERSAL DESIGN FOR THE HOME

QUARRY

UNIVERSAL DESIGN FOR THE HOME

Great Looking, Great Living Design
for All Ages, Abilities, and Circumstances

Wendy A. Jordan

BEVERLY MASSACHUSETTS

QUARRY BOOKS

08 Dec 30
B + t
2499(1749)

First published in the United States of America by Quarry Books, a member of
Quayside Publishing Group
100 Cummings Center
Suite 406-L
Beverly, Massachusetts 01915-6101
Telephone: (978) 282-9590
Fax: (978) 283-2742
www.quarrybooks.com

Library of Congress Cataloging-in-Publication Data
Jordan, Wendy Adler, 1946-
Universal design for the home : barrier-free living for all generations / by Wendy A. Jordan.
p. cm.
ISBN 1-59253-381-7
1. Universal design—United States. 2. Dwellings—Barrier-free design—United States. I. Title.
NA2547.J56 2008
728.087'3—dc22

2007032663
CIP

ISBN-13: 978-1-59253-381-7
ISBN-10: 1-59253-381-7

10 9 8 7 6 5 4 3 2

Design: Collaborated, Inc.
Cover images: Thomas McConnell/Through the Lens Management/Stewart Davis AIA, CG&S Design-Build, (top, left); Renovation Design Group LLC, (top, right); James J. Pirkl, FIDSA, (middle, left); Chris Green/UniversalDesign.com, (lower, right); Dennis Anderson/ Erickson Zebroski Design Group, Inc./Randall Whitehead Lighting, Inc., (bottom, left); icons, Michael Wanke

Printed in Singapore

DEDICATION

To Betsy and Arthur, who
searched for a book like this one

CONTENTS

HOME TOURS: WHOLE-HOUSE DESIGNS 140

Master Planning • A New Home Standard • Small Apartment, Big Appeal
Luxury Living • Independence by Design • Family-Style Ranch House
Top-Flight Lifestyle • Aging Gracefully

UNIVERSAL DESIGN RESOURCES 188

Guidelines and Regulations • Codes and Standards • Specialists • Information
Resources • Manufacturers

▲ Angled wall sections, rather than confining walls, define spaces in this stylish, open plan, aided by contrasting floor, wall, and ceiling materials that distinguish and define the areas. A montage of built-in box cabinets displays artwork without encumbering floor space. The black fireplace and raised hearth are easy to see, easy to use, and effective as a design element.

INTRODUCTION

Universal design is coming of age. Once little known and even less understood, it is taking on, as befits its name, universal appeal. And for good reason; there are so many stylish, beautiful, good-sense universal design applications that choosing them has become a "why not?" rather than a "why?" decision.

Until now, the growing interest in universal design has outpaced the availability of information and design ideas. I became acutely aware of this gap a few years ago when my friends were preparing to build their universal design house. They scoured bookstores and the Internet to find design ideas, product leads, and guidelines for the layman. They were frustrated at every turn. Yet, even as they searched, the universal design field continued to generate more wonderful designs and great innovations.

I wrote this book to bridge the divide. In it, homeowners, as well as their architects, designers, remodelers, and builders, can find the information and inspiration to produce universal design homes tailored to their preferences and needs. Inside, you'll find design principles; project profiles, and photo galleries that illustrate effective designs; examples of the wide array of products now available; and a ton of great ideas. Lists of universal design specifications for the projects are easy to locate (of course), and Spotlights have been trained on particular areas of concern.

Chapter One introduces the universal design approach and shows how it works throughout the house. Subsequent chapters are dedicated to the kitchen, bath, and indoor-outdoor areas, which abound in universal design applications. The Home Tours chapter celebrates designs that put it all together in stylish, accessible residences.

The back of this book is a goldmine of resources—a digest of universal design guidelines, a directory of universal design information sources, contact information for the talented designers in the book, and a list of dozens of manufacturers that make ingenious and beautiful universal design products.

If you are looking for the tools and ideas to design a great-looking, great-living universal design home—a home for everyone—you've come to the right place.

◀ The white and green features and the splash of decorative tiles do more than beautify the room; they help organize the space and provide visual cues.

THE UNIVERSAL DESIGN ADVANTAGE

Sometimes an idea comes along that is so good we wonder how we ever did without it. Universal design is one such idea. The concept crystallized out of the desire to make products and places safe and accessible for everyone—the elderly and the very young, the handicapped and those with physical or other challenges, short people, tall people, and everyone in between. Architect Ron Mace, who coined the term *universal design* and launched the Center for Universal Design at North Carolina State University in the 1980s, summed up the broad scope when he defined universal design as "the design of products and environments to be usable by all people, to the greatest extent possible, without the need for adaptation or specialized design."

At first, much of the focus in universal design was on public places. Some of the universal design options for homes seemed institutional, too "different." Many were ugly, off-putting. If homeowners had a choice, they steered clear of these early designs.

Now the picture is far different. Public interest in universal design has caught fire, igniting an energetic effort by designers and manufacturers to provide fresh, attractive designs for residential use. They have had great success. Today, universal design features blend seamlessly into home designs, drawing little attention to themselves, yet making the designs much better. The importance of universal design is clear, and its value in home design is as fundamental as the ABCs. Well-planned universal design homes are accessible, or barrier-free. They're beautiful, and they are comfortable for all.

Growing in Place

Universal design is a gift to the elderly and to people with physical challenges, such as visual problems, hearing problems, arthritis, or limited mobility, enabling them to enjoy handsome, safe homes that are the envy of their neighbors. Growing numbers of active adults—especially baby boomers—also are choosing homes with the universal design advantage. Why? One reason is that they are easy, attractive places in which to live. Another is that they are adaptable quarters where the residents can "age in place," staying in their homes and living independently even if they develop health or mobility issues in the future.

Some homeowners find themselves in the "sandwich generation," caring for their own children as well as live-in parents or other older relatives. For these families, universal design is ideal. Likewise, it's a smart way to prepare homes that elderly people, handicapped people, or young children may visit.

Many young families gravitate to universal design homes simply because they make bright, open, and well-planned living environments. Others will bless their universal design residences the next time they are home recovering from an injury.

Levels of Advantage

Of course, different people have different circumstances and goals for their homes. Currently, four tiers of design exist to meet that range of needs. Universal design is the most inclusive, since its aim is to accommodate everyone. Accessible design focuses more narrowly, zeroing in on an individual with a disability and addressing that person's particular needs for a barrier-free home. Another approach, adaptable design, plans ahead by incorporating features that may not be accessible now, but are ready for modification if accessibility becomes necessary. The fourth level of design, called visitability, prepares the main floor of a home for visitors with limited mobility; in a visitable home, wheelchair users can enter the house with ease, and comfortably use the living spaces and guest rooms on the main floor.

The terms *universal design* and *accessible* are used interchangeably in this book, but the projects shown meet the universal design standard. Keep in mind that universal design is a work in progress, with an ever-expanding body of ideas. In a few cases, modifications are noted that would add universal design value to already excellent examples. In other cases, creative design ideas are pointed out in rooms where not every feature is compatible with universal design.

By the Book

Laws, regulations, and codes ensure that public and commercial facilities, as well as some multifamily dwellings, meet established standards of accessibility. In most locations, these design specifications are not required for single-family houses and are mandated for only some multi-family and townhouse units. (Check which rules apply in your jurisdiction.) Still, they offer helpful benchmarks for home design. A digest of relevant rules from some of the major American standards has been included in the back of this book.

SPOTLIGHT

The Essence of Universal Design

There's no limit to the creative possibilities for making a home easy and safe to use, but the design should include at least these twenty universal design components.

- At least one home entry that has no steps

- Flat or very low thresholds at doorways

- An open plan with wide doorways, halls, and passageways

- At least a 5-foot (1.5 m)-diameter clear turning space in rooms

- A plan that accommodates one-story living now, or can be adapted easily for this later

- If the house has more than one story, stairs that are low and deep, with handrails on both sides; if possible, include an elevator or the space for one

- Light switches lower than standard and electrical outlets higher than standard, so they are easy for all to reach

- Easy-grip door, faucet, and drawer hardware, such as lever, C-shape, and D-shape handles

- Appliances designed and placed for convenient use from a standing or seated position

- Controls for appliances, heating, air-conditioning, and other equipment that are easy to reach, see, understand, and operate

- Plenty of lighting throughout the house, including natural light, ambient lighting, and task lights

- Easy-to-operate windows, such as casements, awnings, and remote control units

- Generous counters in the kitchen, bathroom, and wherever a tabletop would be handy

- Work surfaces at various heights that are accessible for various users, standing or seated

- A roomy shower with a wide entry and an easy-to-negotiate threshold

- Chair-height toilets

- Grab bars or other handholds in the bathroom and elsewhere

- Reachable storage, including low cabinets, full-extension drawers, open shelves, and adjustable shelves and rods

- Smooth, firm, slip-resistant flooring

- Low-maintenance systems, materials, and finishes

The first step in planning your universal design home is to make a list of goals. Who lives in the house, and who will be visiting it? How old are they? How tall? How dexterous or sure footed? What physical limitations or problems do they have? How do these factors affect how comfortably and safely they can function in the house? How long do you want to stay in the house, and how might your needs change during that time?

As you evaluate your needs, it's helpful to consider what universal design is intended to achieve. The following objectives were articulated in the 1990s by a group of experts assembled by the Center for Universal Design. They drafted seven "Principles of Universal Design," which set standards applied by designers around the world in projects and products that are easy, pleasant, and safe for everyone to use.

1. Equitable Use

The design works for everyone equally, preferably without separate features for certain users. Nobody should be stigmatized, and all should have equal provisions for safety, security, and privacy.

2. Flexibility in Use

The design suits a wide range of abilities and preferences, including a choice in methods of use. Flexible designs anticipate the needs of people who are right handed or left handed, for example, and people who may need more time to complete a task.

3. Simple and Intuitive Use

The design is easy for all to understand. It should make sense and be easy to use, even for someone without experience, reading ability, or language skill.

▲ Built-ins, compact furniture clusters, and diverse ceiling treatments define the living, dining, conversation, and kitchen spaces in this great room, leaving wide swaths of smooth wood floor for circulation. Recessed cabinets and a flush-front fireplace keep the path clear to the screened porch, where sliding glass entry doors and sliding screen doors assure easy indoor/outdoor passage. The angled white ceiling helps project natural light far into the great room.

4. Perceptible Information

Information needed to distinguish or use a design or product is communicated clearly to all. That means good color contrast and multiple, easy-to-use ways of communicating, such as images, words, and textures.

5. Tolerance for Error

The design anticipates accidents and minimizes hazards, by shielding dangerous elements, providing warnings, and incorporating foolproof features.

6. Low Physical Effort

The design can be used efficiently, comfortably, and with minimal effort. In other words, people should be able to use the design without a lot of bending, straining, exertion, or repetitive action.

7. Size and Space for Approach and Use

The design incorporates the size and space needed for every user to function well, regardless of size, posture, or mobility. Tall or short, standing or seated, alone or with an assistant, everyone should be able to see, reach, and comfortably use the features in a design area.

Inspired Spaces

In the design of a home, these principles influence everything from the floor plan to the landscaping to the door handles. Entering a house, circulating from room to room, functioning in a room, and enjoying the outdoors should be easy, efficient, and barrier free. The features of a space—cabinets and closet rods, appliances and office equipment, sinks, tubs and showers, seating and work surfaces, doorways and windows—should be safe and accessible for everyone. Flooring and lighting as well as colors and patterns should be chosen with an eye toward safety.

All this can be done without forfeiting style. Indeed, universal design can add luxury and flair. This book presents a wealth of great ideas for every part of the house. Use it as a resource and a source of inspiration as you shape your own universal design home.

▼ This hospitable dining room features a wide entry and graceful, easy-grasp door handles. Windows, glass doors, and a skylight fill the room with natural light; the chandelier, recessed fixtures, and tall table lamps assure broad, shadow-free evening light. With grips at floor level, the windows are easy to open from a seated position.

Remove the Barriers

New homes and additions generally offer the most latitude for incorporating universal design because they are "clean slates." But don't underestimate the power of remodeling. To gain more circulation room in the living area and kitchen, the owners of this house—one of whom has limited mobility—thought they needed to ante up for an addition. Architect Ann Robinson, of Renovation Design Group, showed them a better, and less expensive, solution: She rearranged the space they already had.

She removed a wall that limited circulation in the living area, exchanging the boxed-off living and family rooms for an airy great room with plenty of space to move around. The wall was load bearing, but Robinson was unworried; in place of the wall, she inserted an overhead beam supported by smart-looking columns, even adding a couple of non-supporting columns to complete the symmetry. By reorganizing the kitchen and replacing the peninsula with an island, Robinson created clear circulation paths in and around the kitchen and breakfast room.

The homeowners also wanted a better integration of indoor and outdoor living spaces. Robinson solved that part of the puzzle by removing the big masonry fireplace that hogged the wall between living area and deck. She filled the wall with a sweep of large windows to bring light and views indoors. Wide, flat-threshold double doors connect the deck with the living area.

Oh, and the homeowners still have a fireplace. The space-efficient built-in cabinetry on an inside wall of the great room incorporates a fireplace insert.

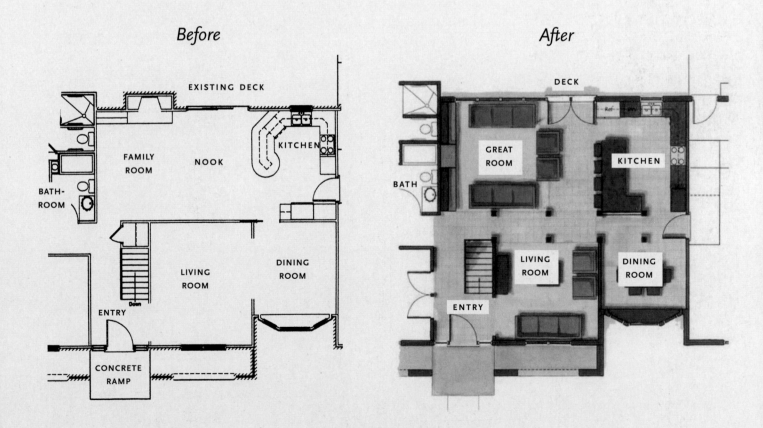

Before

After

THE ULTIMATE LIVABLE HOME

Even before construction began, Rosemarie Rossetti, Ph.D., and Mark Leder's new house was breaking new ground. Designed to accommodate the petite, 4-foot 2-inch (1.27 m)-tall Rossetti, a wheelchair user since a bicycling accident, and her 6-foot 4-inch (1.9 m)-tall husband, it reflects a wide spectrum of considerations, from the practical aspects of day-to-day living to the importance of aesthetics. But the project is not only for Rossetti and Leder; it was planned for the public as well. The product of a team effort by the homeowners, Patrick Manley of the Manley Architecture Group, plus other design specialists, building professionals, and sponsoring suppliers and manufacturers, the house is being called the Universal Design Living Laboratory. It is a home that now and over time will demonstrate some of the most effective ideas in residential universal design.

For Rossetti and Leder, the one-story 3,500-square-foot (1,067.5 sq m) house is a residence and headquarters for two home-based businesses. At the heart of the plan is a spacious living area with smooth, open circulation flow from great room to kitchen to dining area. In the kitchen, a space-efficient lineup of cooking and cleanup centers incorporates legroom for a seated user. The kitchen island has counters at two heights for standing or sitting, food preparation or eating. For easy access, the dishwasher is raised, some wall cabinets are set low, higher cabinets have pull-down shelves, and drawers and pullout shelves run on full-extension glides.

A large pantry is well positioned between the kitchen and two garages, where it doubles as a mudroom and a grocery drop-off point. Lined with low shelves and higher pull-down shelves, the room also houses two easy-to-reach freezer drawers to supplement the side-by-side refrigerator in the kitchen, and shortens the trip from grocery bag to freezer. It made sense to locate the message center here, too. On their way to or from the car, Rossetti and Leder can stop by the telephone desk to check for voice mail.

Another garage door leads to the elevator area. Larger than a standard residential elevator, this cab has room for a wheelchair and carts, allowing Rossetti to transport business inventory to and from the basement.

Separate Offices

For privacy and quiet, the two home offices are on opposite sides of the living space. Rossetti's is next to the laundry area so that she can "multitask" during the workday. A soundproof wall keeps the machine noise from penetrating her workspace. Leder's office is by the guest room. Both offices have large closets and are near bathrooms, so they would work equally well as bedrooms.

To consolidate circulation and make the most productive use of space, Manley eliminated almost all hallways. The area between the master suite and the center of the house provides a way to get from here to there, but it's no ordinary hall. A full 4 feet (1.2 m) wide and lined with bookshelves, it functions as a library. Cookbooks go on the shelves near the kitchen, and work-related books are convenient to Rossetti's office at the other end of the space. Thanks to the two-sided fireplace between the great room and library, Rossetti and Leder can sit by the fire and read.

The master suite flows from a tranquil corner bedroom to a large bathroom and dressing room. Wide doorways and generous floor areas facilitate use of the space, while unobtrusive sliding and pocket doors between rooms and within the bathroom can be closed for privacy. A wall of glass block fills the bathing areas—indeed, the whole bathroom—with natural light and also ensures privacy. Another glass block wall carries the light through to an adjacent room that has a lower sink for a seated user, and a chair-height commode. This is Rossetti's bathroom compartment, but when company comes it can be closed off from the master bath and used as a powder room.

Maximum Light

Skylights, sun tunnels, large windows, and a hatband of clerestories bring natural light into every area of the house. Perimeter lights reflect off the barrel-vaulted great room ceiling to lend atmosphere and clarity; recessed can lights illuminate circulation areas, and task lights enhance workstations in the kitchen, bathrooms, and offices.

This universal design house saves energy in more ways than one. Durable features such as the tile and hardwood flooring, and the quartz countertops and shower stalls don't require much elbow grease to maintain. There are no gutters or downspouts, so they never have to be cleaned; rainwater is piped away from the house. With deep eaves and broad north and south sides, the house is shaded to reduce air-conditioning demand in the summer months, and enjoys passive solar gain in the winter.

GREAT IDEA

The Clothing Room

The tiresome job of carting clothing back and forth from laundry room to closet has been eliminated in this house. How? The laundry area and closet have been merged into one large room. One end of the laundry section is arranged in a practical sequence, from utility sink (1) to washer and dryer (2), to pull-down drying rack. A wall-mounted ironing board (3) folds down and can be set at two heights for use standing or seated. Cabinets (4), low closet rods (5), and higher pull-down rods line the rest of the room. A large central island (6) packs in more dresser drawers; the top can be used for folding clothes, packing luggage, or laying out the outfit for the day.

36-inch (91.44 cm)-wide doorways

Flat thresholds

Garage floor sloped for drainage away from at-grade entry

Balanced light

Casement windows

Lever handles and C-shaped drawer pulls

Adjustable shelves and closet rods

Raised outlets, lowered light switches

Kitchen counters at multiple heights—30, 34, 36, and 42 inches (76.2, 86.4, 91.4, and 106.6 cm)

Knee room under sinks, cooktop, some counters

Pot filler at cooktop

In-counter steamer with water drain at cooktop

Side-mounted faucets

Side-by-side refrigerator/freezer

Oven with side-hinged door

Accessible-height appliances with front-mounted controls

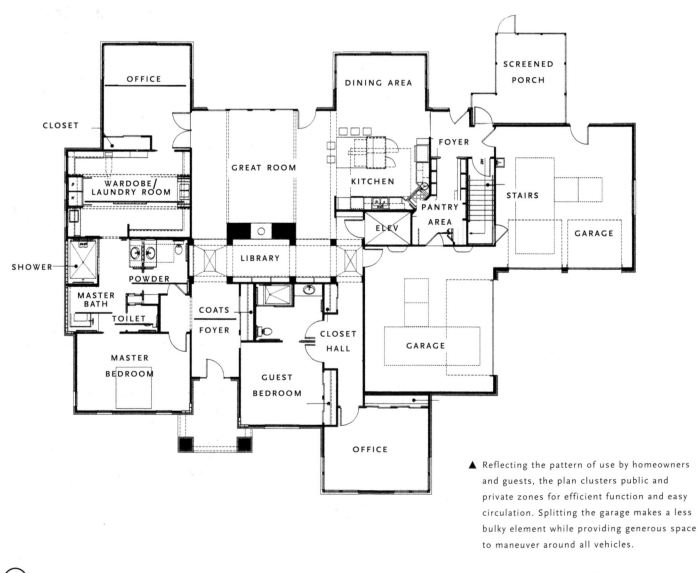

▲ Reflecting the pattern of use by homeowners and guests, the plan clusters public and private zones for efficient function and easy circulation. Splitting the garage makes a less bulky element while providing generous space to maneuver around all vehicles.

Accessible height cabinets, with 9-inch (22.9 cm) toekick space

Freezer drawers

Curbless shower

Adjustable handheld shower spray

Shower bench

Chair-height toilets

Grab bars

Front-loaded washer and dryer

Adjustable pull-down ironing board

Elevator

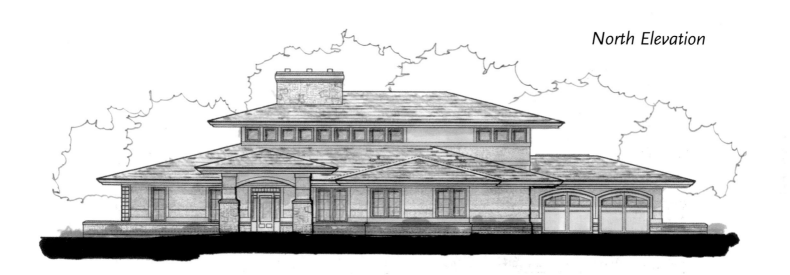

North Elevation

▲ Spread across a level site, the one-story, Prairie Style house has a horizontal rhythm punctuated by high clerestory windows that admit natural light from all sides. The house has no gutters or downspouts to maintain; deep eaves help shade the house and channel rainwater away from the at-grade flat-threshold entries to a fishpond and drainage creek. The front portico extends over the driveway to shield visitors from the elements.

SP⊙TLIGHT

The Incredible, Changeable Room

It used to be that homeowners conformed to the dictates of their houses, furnishing the living room, dining room, and guest room as such, even if it meant those rooms were rarely used. Then the tables turned. Homeowners took charge, converting dining rooms to playrooms, living rooms to dens, guest rooms to home offices. Recognizing the need for adaptable spaces, designers and home builders have gone a step further, including in their plans flex rooms, or rooms with the built-in flexibility to be used for whatever purposes suit the homeowners.

Flex rooms are ideal for universal design homes. They accommodate various uses now, and can be changed easily to meet different needs later. First-floor flex rooms are especially worthwhile, expanding the options for families with children, for adults looking to stay in their homes and age in place, and for homeowners who anticipate that elderly relatives may move in at some point.

A room that begins as a nursery can evolve into a playroom and then a study as the children grow. A hobby room can morph into a guest room, or vice versa. A library can become a home office. A sitting area or exercise room can be transformed into a caregiver apartment.

The Basics

For maximum flexibility, the room needs wide doorways, flat thresholds, good lighting, and enough space for easy circulation, even when it is set up for various uses. A room that might become a bedroom needs enough clear wall area for placement of the bed and other furnishings. Built-in storage

should be accessible for all, whether standing or seated.

The location of flex rooms is important. If a den or dining room, for example, is envisioned as a future bedroom, it should be outside the center of the living space but close, if not connected, to a bathroom. In a master suite, both the bedroom and the flex room should have direct access to closets and the bathroom; that way, if the flex room becomes a bedroom for one homeowner or a station for a caregiver, both rooms will enjoy privacy and convenience. A room that might serve as an office or apartment works best along an outside wall, for natural light, and near an entry—perhaps a secondary entry that could be a private entrance for a relative or caregiver.

Running plumbing and high-capacity wiring through the walls multiplies the options for a flex room. Prepping the room in this way adds to the initial construction cost, but saves much more money later by simplifying the remodeling when it's time to adapt the room. With pipes in place, you can add a bathroom or a kitchenette to create a self-sufficient apartment, or set up a laundry room in an accessible new location. With wiring and outlets lined up, your flex room can to go to work as a home office. If you'd rather have a media room, it's ready to be that, too.

◀ Set apart from the living area and adjacent to a guest bathroom, this den is ready for conversion to a bedroom. The glass double doors that fill the wide, smooth entryway can easily be replaced with solid doors for privacy, and the room already has a private entrance to the bath. High windows will admit light over the bed.

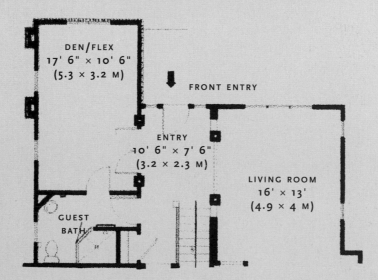

DEN/FLEX
17' 6" × 10' 6"
(5.3 × 3.2 M)

FRONT ENTRY

ENTRY
10' 6" × 7' 6"
(3.2 × 2.3 M)

LIVING ROOM
16' × 13'
(4.9 × 4 M)

GUEST BATH

Gallery

ROOM-TO-ROOM CONNECTIONS

An open floor plan makes it easier to get around in a house. Creative use of color and materials, built-in cabinets and cutouts, and interior windows and doors can organize the space clearly and unrestrictively.

◄ Color and pattern provide spice and spatial orientation here. Nonskid slate tiles cover the hallways, yielding to wood flooring at the wide doorless entries to the office, family room, and kitchen. Wall colors, from the yellow of the halls to the teal of the family room, further identify spaces. Some wall cutouts are display niches; others are interior windows that help spread the light.

▼ Instead of confining walls and doors, a bold flooring montage and commanding fireplace organize this living/dining/kitchen space without presenting obstacles to circulation and room-to-room communication. The mahogany floor strip stylishly marks the dining room boundary and signals the edge of the fireplace wall; a built-in cabinet-column ensemble identifies the opening to the kitchen.

Indoor Ramp

All it takes is one or two stairs to isolate a living area and introduce a safety hazard for young and old. Steps to the sunken living area in this house have been replaced by an interior ramp that winds down gently from the entry. To prevent mishaps, the oak ramp contrasts visually with the lower stone floor, and features a raised edge strip.

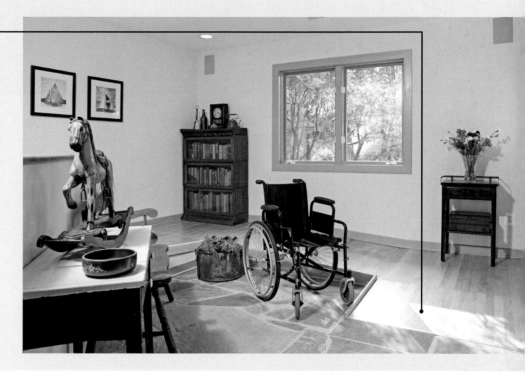

▲ This residential elevator makes the second floor accessible to everyone, and does so without altering the character of the house at all. That's because the elevator access door matches the other doors in the house in both style and size. The location of the elevator honors the house's traffic pattern, too. Whether taking the elevator or climbing the stairs, all arrive at the same place on the second floor landing.

▲ A smooth-track pocket door is the solution when you want to separate rooms where a hinged door would get in the way. A duo of pocket doors is even better. The beauty of paired pocket doors is that they create a large, flat-threshold opening without reducing any surrounding wall or cabinet exposure or access. They can be purchased or custom made to fit any architectural style or part of the house; these traditional-looking French doors add character to the living room and admit light from the sunroom.

Gallery

ENTRYWAYS

An entryway should be prepared for every contingency—a package-laden homeowner, a visitor in a wheelchair, children ducking in from the rain, a stranger at the door. Give it a broad doorway and foyer, seating, a nonslip floor, good lighting, and windows to see out, and it will be ready to go.

◄ The stained glass sidelight by this wide entry door protects privacy while enabling the home-owners to see out. Convenient as a package drop-off or seat, the recessed bench is close to the door yet out of the circulation area; nonslip, waterproof stone tiles provide a safe, low-maintenance floor surface.

▼ This understair cabinet keeps the floor clear of boots, but brings them into easy reach when needed. More low, handy storage is tucked under the built-in bench. The nonskid tiles are just right for a mudroom.

Curving Mudroom Wall

Most mudrooms are messy and cramped. Not only that, but when the door is open, the circulation space becomes even tighter. This gracefully curved wall gets around the problem. It hides the mess from general view, leaves ample floor space in the mudroom, and offers wide access to the living area. The painted wall stands out, aiding in spatial orientation and lending a decorative accent to the back entry. Low shelving and under-bench cabinets help combat clutter.

Gallery

BEDROOMS

Built-in cabinets and sliding doors conserve precious floor space for circulation in the bedroom. Wide doorways extend the smooth flow into adjacent spaces, and well-placed windows make the bedroom cheerful and bright.

▲ Art and utility merge with custom barn-door–style metal doors—one broad, one narrower—that glide aside for a smooth, wide connection between bedroom and bath. Windows sprinkled across the doors spread light between the rooms but protect privacy. Flush with the wall, the built-in cabinets and entertainment system leave the floor space clear. Tall windows and recessed uplights provide generous overall lighting; track lights illuminate task areas.

▶ Featuring a nightstand, storage drawer, and wall-mounted bedside lamp, this custom-crafted bed structure integrates the bedroom furnishings in one stable piece to eliminate the tripping hazards of furniture legs and electrical cords. Constructed of maple with cherry accents, the structure is durable as well as chic.

A Foyer for the Bedroom

A central foyer affords furniture-free maneuvering room in this master suite, with a wide, gracious bedroom entry on one side, a bathroom (not shown) on another, and a closet on a third. Low rods and open, adjustable shelving bring things into reach in the closet.

◀ Windows across two walls, including high units over the bed, provide penetrating, balanced light while respecting privacy. Convenient but out of the circulation path, the accessible, chair-height window seat serves as a bench, tabletop, and storage drawer.

Gallery

STORAGE

The best storage systems bring items into easy reach and keep them organized. It's a bonus when storage units fill underused, accessible spaces around the house, adding function and cutting clutter.

◀ Sports equipment is easy for children to find, reach, and put away in low, rollout bins. The open shelves and low-handled cabinets keep other things organized and accessible for children as well as short and seated people.

GREAT IDEA

Sliding Translucent Doors

Enclosed by semitranslucent tempered glass wall panels, this closet forms a stylish "light box" that radiates a soft glow into the bedroom. The sliding door screens closet contents from view when closed and occupies no floor space when it glides open for access to the closet, which is fitted out with double rods and good-looking adjustable shelving. Hinged glass doors from the same door manufacturer lend design continuity and spread light throughout the apartment.

Gallery

LAUNDRY

Front-loaded machines installed a foot or so off the floor take the bending and straining out of doing the laundry. Integrate the machines into the cabinetry for a convenient, attractive laundry center in the kitchen or bedroom area.

◀ Raised above drawers and inserted into cabinet openings, the washer and dryer are comfortable for the homeowners to use, whether standing or seated. A drying rack makes smart use of the cabinet overhead; the cabinet door recedes to air-dry clothes that have been hung on the pull-down rack.

GREAT IDEA

Convertible Laundry Center

There's no sense using an inviting corner like this only on washday. A desk for paying bills or planning menus makes nice use of the sunny space, which transitions easily into a laundry center. Baskets for sorting wash are accessible on undercounter shelves; clothes can be folded on the desk and counter; and an ironing board emerges from a drawer at a good height for the homeowner to iron while sitting or standing.

Gallery

WORKSTATIONS

Universal design workstations are all about clarity—clear access to the desk and equipment, clear circulation space and legroom, a clearly organized, convenient storage system for supplies, and clear, nonglare lighting.

▶ Installed at chair height, the window seat in this office makes a comfortable bench for all to use and offers a smooth transition for someone in a wheelchair. Shelves under the seat place books and papers within reach; the open cabinet above the desk keeps office supplies organized and at hand.

GREAT IDEA

Computer Bay

Books, pencils, and papers clutter the dining table or kitchen counter at homework time in most family homes. Not in this one, where a crescent-shape desktop lines the window bay. Computer equipment remains ready for action on the work surface, and supplies are close but out of sight in low cabinets camouflaged within the custom columns on each side. The wide-open bay is easily accessed and close to the family area, yet out of the traffic path.

Step-by-Step Stair Planning

When designing stairs, think steady and gentle, wide and light. The idea is to avoid surprises and provide good support every step of the way.

Staircases with a moderate pitch—each riser 6 or 7 inches (15.2 or 17.8 cm) high—provide a gentle, knee-friendly climb that probably won't leave anyone breathless. Broad landings make nice rest spots and, fitted out with a bench, chair, or window seat, become cozy reading nooks or conversation corners.

The staircase can wind its way up but each tread beyond the entry point, including those that round the bends, should be the same size rectangle. What size should that be? At 11 or 12 inches (17.9 or 30.5 cm), the stair is deep enough to give adults a solid foothold. Most codes say stairs should be 3 feet (7.6 cm) wide, but 4 feet (10.2 cm) has the advantage of allowing room for two people—adult and toddler, or homeowner and care provider—to go up side by side. (A straight staircase 4 feet (10.2 cm) wide is broad enough to accommodate a chairlift, too.)

Smart Details

Install strong, well-anchored handrails on both sides of the staircase. Railings that are an inch and a half (3.8 cm) wide and the same distance out from the wall offer a good grip. Solid risers and balusters spaced no more than 4 inches (10.2 cm) apart are safest for small children. It's best to avoid deep overhangs, or nosings, that might cause someone to trip; a well-fastened runner of tight-weave carpeting will solve the nosing problem on existing stairs.

Lighting can add drama as well as safety to stairs. It doesn't matter what combination of lighting you choose, as long as the staircase is lighted fully and evenly. Skylights can bathe an entire staircase in sunlight, as can well-placed nonglare windows. For electric lighting, try overhead fixtures that cast a broad beam, track lights, or other lights regularly spaced along the stairs. Place light switches at both the top and bottom of the staircase; lighted rocker switches are best.

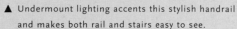

▲ Undermount lighting accents this stylish handrail and makes both rail and stairs easy to see.

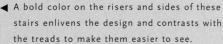

◄ A bold color on the risers and sides of these stairs enlivens the design and contrasts with the treads to make them easier to see.

PRODUCTS FOR THE HOME

▼ This antimicrobial, latex-free attachment converts a round doorknob or faucet control into an easy-grip handle with lever extension. Also available in glow-in-the-dark and bright color models, it is economical, easy to see, and eye-catching for children.

▲ Combine storage components in a closet system that places clothing where it is easy to see and reach. This space-efficient design includes low rods and shelves, an integrated dresser, and shoe cubbies, all with toe space underneath for a seated user.

▲ Install a hinged rod like this to reach the clothes at the top of the closet without the need for a stepstool. The adjustable, twist-and-lock upright post holds the rod securely in place, becoming a handle to pull the rod down.

◄ Tucked between the washer and dryer, this laundry tower incorporates drawers for laundry supplies and an easily reached, pullout rod for air-drying or hanging clothes. Together with the appliances, the tower forms a spacious countertop for folding clothes.

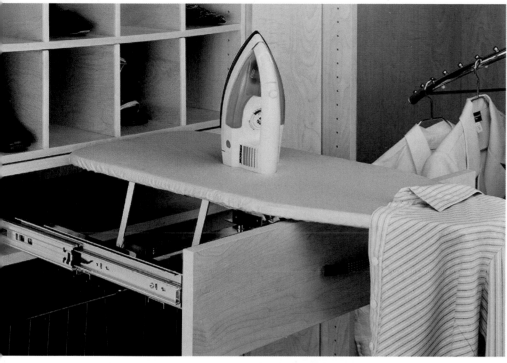

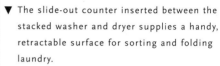

An ironing board that folds into a drawer space can be installed at any height, depending on whether you prefer ironing in a chair, on a stool, or standing up. This one is in the closet, where shirts can be ironed and hung up without an extra trip.

▼ The slide-out counter inserted between the stacked washer and dryer supplies a handy, retractable surface for sorting and folding laundry.

▲ Sorting laundry can be done efficiently from a standing or seated position with the help of this custom-installed storage suite, which clusters the hamper and drawers close to the washer and dryer. The wire basket drawers keep folded items put away but in view; the drawers extend fully for easy access.

▲ Most residential elevators come in a choice of designs and finishes. The wood door and interior of this elevator match the trim, flooring, and other doors in the house; the paneling complements the house's classic style.

▲ Upgrading to a glass door and cab wall adds light and contemporary flair to this elevator. To capitalize on the design, the architect inserted a curved glass wall in the elevator shaft.

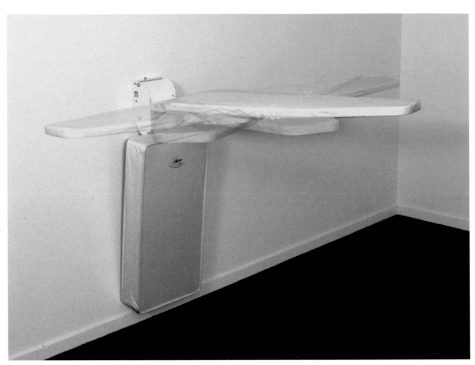

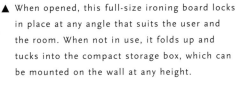

▲ When opened, this full-size ironing board locks in place at any angle that suits the user and the room. When not in use, it folds up and tucks into the compact storage box, which can be mounted on the wall at any height.

▲ A handheld remote control unit operates the venetian blinds attached to these roof windows, so the light can be refocused or reduced to cut glare.

▲ Especially well-suited for remodeling, this elevator fits into an existing space with minimal retrofitting because it has low clearance overhead and rests on the main floor, requiring no pit underneath. Instead, it operates with a counterweight chain drive or a hydraulic system that can be installed elsewhere. The elevator comes in three sizes and several finishes.

▼ The electrochromic glass in these energy-efficient skylights can be darkened to reduce glare. You can activate the darkening process at the touch of a button or set a timer to darken the glass at the same time each day.

▲ A mahogany look-alike made of low-maintenance fiberglass, this 3-foot (.9 m)-wide door can be customized with glass inserts, sidelights, and transoms in different styles to add light and let homeowners see who is at the door. An accessible $\frac{1}{2}$-inch (1.3 cm) -high public access sill is available.

▲ Hinged patio doors with stylish lever handles come in a variety of widths, heights, and colors. The durable, fiberglass doors feature low-E glass for temperature control and energy efficiency, with an adjustable sill or low threshold option.

▲ Bring fresh air into the house with an operable skylight. This one opens by remote control; a sensor automatically closes the skylight if it gets rainy outside.

▼ Instead of the dark, cavernous cabinets typical of most wet bars, these full-extension gliding shelves with protective rims bring bottles and cans into clear view and easy reach. Custom configured for the space, the shelves are made of strong Baltic birch.

▲ Tap on an activator or push the button on a remote to lower these motorized cabinets into easy reach. The fiberglass cabinets, made in several standard sizes, come with adjustable shelves; apply your own doors and face frames to match the other cabinets in the room.

▶ Good looking and strong, these handgrips offer security and style at doorways and stairs; by desks, counters, and work areas; and at the tub, shower, toilet, and vanity in the bathroom. The 9-inch (22.9 cm) grips come in a choice of finishes.

▲ Use a residential dumbwaiter to transport groceries, firewood, trash, laundry, packages, breakables, and other items from floor to floor. Available in several sizes, this wood dumb-waiter comes with a shelf and rolltop door. Custom size steel units also are available.

▼ Give the manufacturer your own design for the interior of your home elevator or choose from the wide range of standard offerings, such as this elegant model with walnut strips inset in raised, bird's-eye maple panels.

▲ Sealed between glass panels, these door blinds are raised, lowered, and tilted for light control and security by pushing accessible buttons integrated into the frame. The full and half-door blinds never need to be cleaned, and there are no cords to become tangled or present a safety hazard for children.

◄ Small, louvered lights recessed in the exterior wall clearly illuminate the steps without causing glare. The lights, which come in a range of colors, feature tempered glass, and are suitable for wet areas.

FIVE-STAR KITCHENS

Versatility makes a good kitchen great—and universal design is all about versatility. Kitchens have become much more than rooms where the cook fixes dinner; today, they are family gathering places, guest entertainment centers, and areas where two or more people often work together to prepare meals. We want kitchens that are comfortable, convenient, safe, and well-equipped for all these activities and for everyone: children and grandparents, short and tall adults, seated and standing people. Universal design makes it possible in one efficient space.

Kitchens do not have to be large to be versatile; in fact, when they are too large, they can become unwieldy. In a universal design kitchen, allocation of space is more important than size. Passageways should be wide and straight, allowing a free flow within the kitchen and into adjoining rooms. An open center, at least 5 feet (1.5 m) in diameter, gives everyone in the kitchen, including wheelchair users, room to move around. Include enough open space at each workstation for people to use appliances and open cabinets with ease, and spread the work centers around the room so that everyone can share the kitchen without getting in each other's way.

ABC's of Kitchen Design

A U-shaped kitchen, or an L-shaped design with an island bridging the sides, can do a nice job of distributing the main work zones—cooking, cleanup, refrigerator, food preparation—around the room, giving each zone elbow room yet keeping the areas close enough for convenient meal preparation. Another advantage of these configurations is that they incorporate lots of countertop area, and in any kitchen, the more counters the better. Counters with rounded edges, blunted corners, and even molded grips are best.

For the most convenience, include generous counter space on both sides of the sink, cooktop, and oven, and by the open side of the refrigerator. Making the counters in the cooking areas the same height as the cooktop and as the middle rack of the oven enables the user to transfer heavy pots with little or no lifting. Likewise, the counter between cooking areas and sink should be one height, so that cooks can slide pots between them. A heat-resistant countertop material such as granite or solid surfacing is the best choice in these areas.

Elsewhere around the kitchen, variety in countertop heights adds flexibility. Low counters with legroom beneath work well as food-preparation stations for seated users, as well as desks, homework spots, eating areas, and places to knead dough. Tall standing users welcome high counters for slicing vegetables and other close work.

To conserve open space, install pullout cutting boards and counters. Secured on drawer gliders, they make sturdy work surfaces at a comfortable height for seated users. Pullout shelves under the oven and microwave provide convenient landing places for pots. For the ultimate in instant countertop customization, include a rolling cabinet in the plan, or mount the kitchen island on casters.

Convenient Cooking

Instead of a one-piece range, opt for a separate cooktop and wall oven, which offer more flexibility in installation. Choose a cooktop with a smooth surface, to facilitate sliding pots on and off; staggered front and back burners, for clear access; and easy-to-see front-mounted controls.

Place it in a counter with clear space beneath for a seated user, and position the oven—or the lower one if two are stacked—above floor level and no higher than shoulder height for a seated cook. Side-hinged oven doors offer easiest access, but pull-down doors are fine if they are easy to open and rest above lap level in the open position.

Plan the cleanup area, like the cooking zone, with different users in mind. Raise the dishwasher several inches above floor level so that the top rack aligns with the counter and users—seated or standing—can reach both racks without a lot of bending. Provide legroom under the sink for a seated person, even if nobody needs to sit at the kitchen sink now,

▲ Style goes hand in hand with convenience in universal design kitchens. Arranged across one end of the family room area, the kitchen is organized as an efficient work area but feels open, airy, and connected. The colorful tile backsplash and counter edge strips form striking visual locators. Equally practical is the flooring border. The open shelving is dynamic and accessible. A mix of counter heights, rolling carts, pullout work surfaces, and an adjustable sink suit a variety of users and functions. Matching cabinetry gives the kitchen, computer area, and adjacent laundry a unified look.

GREAT IDEA

Steps Away

Small children can't reach the kitchen sink, and a stool parked in front of the sink becomes an obstacle for everyone else. What to do? One idea is to attach a slim fold-down stool to the inside of the cabinet door under the sink; the stools are sold by cabinet accessory companies. Or create a pullout step like this one in the toe kick. It is sturdy, easy to use, and virtually invisible when put away.

either by creating an open area with a protective panel or insulation over the rear-mounted pipes or installing a removable cabinet unit. To save money and hassle, be sure to run the kitchen flooring into the opening, even if it will be covered for now by cabinetry. For a seated user, the sink should be about 4 inches (10.2 cm) lower than standard counter height. It's easier for everyone to reach into a shallow, say, 6-inch (15.2 cm)-deep sink, and the shallow sink allows more legroom. Single-lever faucets tend to be easiest to use for both young and old.

Side-by-side refrigerators put both refrigerator and freezer sections in convenient reach of all users, and have the added advantage of absorbing little floor space when the door is open. Stow small appliances in counter-height appliance garages, or mount some on retractable shelves.

All-Out Storage

Design the storage system throughout the kitchen for maximum capacity and clear, open access to items, using full-extension drawers and shelves, pullout cabinets, vertical slats, adjustable shelving, and such storage wonders as pull-down, fold-out, and revolving cabinet inserts that bring otherwise hidden or inaccessible items into reach. Attach the top cabinets at a lower-than-standard 15 inches (38.1 cm) above the counter to bring them into reach, and carve out a deep toe kick under lower cabinets to provide wheelchair toe space. Put storage where it's most convenient—dishes near the dishwasher, cooking utensils near the cooktop, knives by the food-preparation station—to streamline tasks and minimize moving

around. Capture every available space, from narrow dividers between cabinets—a great place for vertical pullouts—to slim shelves along the countertop backsplash. And don't ignore the space under raised appliances; they make handy spots for cookware drawers.

Contrasting colors for flooring, kick plates, cabinets and counters enliven the kitchen, while providing organization and visual clarity. Of course, bright, nonglare lighting is a must. A mix of broad-reaching ambient lighting, task lighting, and natural light from windows and skylights is the recipe for safe, satisfying sessions in the kitchen.

▲ Recessing this corner cooking center makes the counters on each side especially accessible. The big, bright controls for the range top are easy to see and turn, and lighting on the angled, unobtrusive hood helps users monitor what's cooking. Open shelves keep spices and utensils at hand; pots and pans are stowed in drawers right under the cooktop.

LOOKING BACK, PLANNING AHEAD

Architect John Salmen and his wife, Ann Scher, fulfilled two seemingly conflicting goals when they bought and rebuilt a rundown 1910 bungalow. Looking back to the house's early nineteenth century Arts and Crafts architectural style for inspiration, they created a homey environment that has old-fashioned charm. Looking forward, they incorporated universal design features that will allow them to live comfortably in the house for decades to come.

The kitchen melds vintage and progressive styles with particular artfulness. Simple cabinetry and quartersawn oak floor, traditional-looking windows, warm colors and naturally contrasting cherry accents, a broad island that looks like a kitchen table, and a decorative motif that evokes an Arts and Crafts window pattern—all this together paints the portrait of a warm old-style kitchen. Salmen, a universal design specialist, partnered with universal design expert Jane Langmuir to integrate easy-use elements into the plan with such finesse that many are hard to spot.

Much of the storage, for instance, is under the counters or in shelves along the backsplash where items are easy to see and access. Instead of a cramped pantry closet that might be difficult to negotiate with a walker or wheelchair,

they installed full-extension drawers and vertical, pullout shelving units that bring supplies into the open. The base cabinets rest on short legs that lend an old-fashioned look while forming a deep toe kick space that is wheelchair friendly. And a cherry-topped cart with bins for trash and compost can be rolled out of the island to make legroom for someone to sit at the counter.

Cabinet to Go

At the boundary between kitchen and hall, they crafted a cabinet that looks like a hutch, with two-sided glass display case above and drawers below. In fact, the lower cabinet is a tea cart with a removable serving tray top and a pullout toaster oven shelf. Like the trash cart, it can be used to enhance a work area and also to transport items, whether around the kitchen or into the elevator to for breakfast in bed upstairs. With interior lighting and glass shelves, the upper cabinet makes glassware easy to find. A mix of drawer and door pulls gives the kitchen an informal, home-grown look, and all are easy to grip.

Side-by-side refrigerators put freezer and refrigerator sections within reach of most people, but Salmen chose a refrigerator with a bottom freezer. The decision involved a tradeoff: gain compartments that hold larger items, but require some people to stoop more to use the freezer. For added convenience and accessibility, Salmen installed two undercounter refrigerator drawers on the other side of the room, close to the sink, island food-preparation area, and microwave. He installed a pair of undercounter dishwasher drawers, too, putting one on each side of the cleanup sink rather than stacking them, so they are equally accessible.

◀ Reminiscent of an old-fashioned kitchen table, the island complements the warm, Arts and Crafts styling of the room. With a cooktop at one corner, a food-preparation/drink sink at another, an eating counter along the back, and a suite of efficient storage—including a removable trash/recycling cart—it's actually a modern, multifunctional kitchen component.

GREAT IDEA

Windows *and* Cabinets

What will it be, lots of cabinets or lots of windows? Deciding what to put on the outside wall of the kitchen need not be an either-or proposition. A bank of casement windows runs nearly the full length of the wall, providing privacy and tranquil views while pouring sunlight and fresh air into the kitchen and the family room beyond. The windows are big, but they occupy only the top half of the wall, leaving room for plentiful storage, from shelves to easy-open cabinetry to metal rods for hanging utensils, metal racks and baskets, dish towels, and paper towels.

Counters at assorted heights, from the 29-inch (73.7 cm)-high cherry breakfast board along the back of the island to the 34-inch (86.4 cm)-high island top and the 36-inch (91.4 cm)-high integrated drain board at the cleanup sink, allow Salmen and his wife to sit in the kitchen or work standing without a lot of bending. The kitchen counters are low-maintenance soapstone and stainless steel.

Instead of a bulky range with a low, awkward-to-use oven, Salmen selected a wall oven and centered it 42 inches (106.7 cm) above the floor, where a cook can use it comfortably whether standing or seated. He installed two cooktops that suit different purposes. In the island, and handy to the food-preparation center and breakfast bar, a smooth-surface induction cooktop is convenient for light cooking. A larger cooktop for full meal preparation integrates an electric grill and a gas wok burner; it's strategically located next to the pullout spray, drain board, and sink to simplify cleanup.

▶ The dark tone of the counters and cooktops contrasts with the light cabinetry, providing a visual cue to identify the work surfaces. Cherry rails at the island and the cleanup zone pick up the wood tones of the room and furnish a handhold on both sides of the workspace.

▼ Stacked refrigerator drawers share easy-access undercounter space with a storage/tea cart that transports an auxiliary work surface and an extra microwave to wherever they are needed.

- Easy-grip drawer and cabinet handles

- Single-lever faucets

- Instant hot and cold filtered water

- Accessible dishwasher and refrigerator drawers

- Pullout storage

- Removable, under-counter carts

- Varied counter heights

- Extended grab bars

- Easy-to-reach wall oven

- Smooth induction cooktop

- Multipurpose cooktop with controls at front

- Smooth floor and wide circulation space

- High toe kicks

- Well-distributed natural and artificial lighting

ALL IN THE FAMILY

This is a kitchen for everyone in the family. It's as suitable for home cooking as for homework, for go-it-alone endeavors as for group efforts, for rapid cleanup as for creative rearranging. How does it achieve such versatility? The answer is not in the size of the space; at about 12 by 20 feet (3.7 × 6.1 m), the three-sided kitchen is relatively compact. Nor is it in the budget; with mid-price appliances, semicustom cabinets, sheet vinyl flooring, affordable pendant task lights, and basic solid-surface counters, the kitchen is composed largely of standard elements. What sets it apart is the impressive number and variety of work centers integrated cleverly into the streamlined plan to address virtually any scenario a dynamic family might present over time.

Universal design specialist Mary Jo Peterson designed the adaptable, accessible family kitchen as a prototype for General Electric. Using counters of different heights, adding movable surfaces, and doubling up on sinks and ovens, she created multiple work zones that accommodate a variety of users. Storage is distributed around the room for handy access. Simple, attractive color blocks in the flooring visually map the room and cabinet perimeters, while reinforcing the contemporary styling of the room.

A Second Sink

One sink, a double-bowl unit between the dishwasher and a spacious counter with cutout waste chute, completes both cleanup and food-preparation zones. It's an integral part of the refrigerator-range-sink work triangle. And it can be adjusted in height to suit short or tall users; legroom underneath accommodates seated users. A second sink, located at one end of the island, works as a stand-alone food-preparation station. At the same time, it brings water conveniently close to the adjacent cooktop, and

▲ The pullout counter under the wall oven extends far enough to function as an auxiliary workspace, or to provide a sizable transfer surface when the oven is open.

completes an alternate sink-oven-refrigerator work triangle that lets family members share the kitchen without getting in each other's way.

The induction cooktop is user-friendly, too. It reduces burning hazards, because the cooking surface does not get hot, and its smooth surface enables cooks to slide pots on and off with minimal lifting. The cabinet under the cooktop can be used for storage or as legroom for a seated cook.

One oven, mounted conveniently midwall, is a microwave convection model, adaptable for quick or conventional cooking. A pullout board beneath it provides a transfer surface for items going in or out of the oven. The long, strong board doubles as an auxiliary work surface as well, and is low enough for comfortable use by a child or someone in a chair. A second microwave slips neatly into the island, on a shelf by the breakfast table. It

furnishes an auxiliary cooking corner and an inviting booth where family members can pull up a chair to eat breakfast, fix a snack, do homework, or chat.

Versatile Counter- and Tabletops

A continuous, table-height counter bends around from the wall oven to the computer station at one side of the kitchen. The counter binds the computer zone to the kitchen proper, working equally well as a kneading surface for bakers and a place for children and adults to sit and prepare food or do paperwork.

Peterson took versatility a step further in this kitchen, incorporating two movable surfaces into the plan. One is a lightweight cart with two open wire shelves and a smooth top. Parked in the corner pantry, it stores kitchen supplies. Rolled anywhere else in the kitchen, it transports food, dishes, or heavy pots; or contributes an extra, table-height work surface.

Through the Looking Glass

One size usually does not fit all when it comes to positioning a computer monitor. This computer, however, works for the whole family. That's because the monitor rests at a slight tilt inside a glass-topped counter. It reflects no glare, keeps everyone from pulling up too close, and causes every user—from small child to tall adult—to look gently downward, as recommended for ergonomic reasons. Another bonus: With the monitor off the counter and the CPU in a cabinet, the desk is clear and ready for hire as a spillover kitchen workspace.

The second changeable component is the breakfast table. Fit snugly between accessible, open shelves, it looks like a permanent fixture of the island. But with casters inset in two legs, it can be moved easily; with two flat-based legs, it rests securely when in place. Around the island, the card-table-size table creates a work area that's ample for one seated user and large enough for two to share. At the computer center, it broadens the desk, so that family members can spread out a project, or parents can be nearby as the kids do their homework.

▶ Easy-grip controls are grouped at the front of the cooktop, where they are most accessible. Bifold doors move aside for clear access to the open space underneath, which can be used for storage or legroom.

▼ Parked at the island, the breakfast table has a microwave oven close by. With casters in two legs, the table can be moved to where an extra work surface is needed and settled securely into place.

Multiple workstations for different users

Pullout counters and transfer surface at oven

Adjustable sink with legroom for seated user

Rollout shelves, cart, and table

Generous counters at various heights

Side-by-side refrigerator

Raised dishwasher

Smooth, induction cooktop with easy-grip controls

Legroom under cooktop

Undercounter microwave

C-shape handles

Single-lever faucets with pullout spray

Visual cues in floor, counter

DOUBLE EXPOSURE

Now you see it, now you don't. The cabinetry presents a linear profile as it winds around the perimeter of this uncluttered kitchen. When the homeowner is busy preparing a meal, it morphs into a multidimensional work center, with pullout cutting boards and storage units distributed strategically around the room.

One hefty chopping block emerges from behind a flip-down drawer front near the wall oven and microwave. Designers Angie Soulier, of Tandem Design Group, and Sylvia Fernando, International Kitchens, put the board in that location so it can serve a double purpose; it's a heat-resistant staging surface for items going in or out of the ovens and a station where the homeowner, who uses a wheelchair, can draw up to prepare ingredients. Another dual-duty cutting board slides out by the cooktop. A third adds a work surface near the sink and dish-

washer. Because they occupy undercounter drawer space, all the boards are 4 inches (10 cm) below the standard 36-inch (91.4 cm)-high counters. That means they are comfortably placed regardless of whether the user is seated or standing.

Voila: the Coffeemaker

The dynamic cabinetry system includes a variety of rollout shelves that brings equipment and supplies into the open. A pullout platform by the sink houses the trash and recycling bins, and super-slim vertical pullouts keep equipment at hand by the sink and stove. Lazy Susans in corner cabinets spin bottles, cans, and spices into reach. Large drawers bring pots and pans out from the cabinet depths. A roomy appliance garage stores several small appliances neatly out of sight. To use his coffeemaker, the homeowner raises the garage's

tambour door and simply slides the appliance onto the counter; no lifting is needed. At cleanup time, he can open the pocket doors under the sink, slide them out of the way, and pull up to the sink to do dishes.

The cooktop sits in a 30-inch (76.2 cm)-high, table-height counter section, where all burners are easy to see and reach, even from a seated position; generous counter space on both sides let the homeowner move pots on and off the burners without carrying them far.

Even when all the movable parts of this flexible cabinet suite are tucked away, one inventive feature remains in view. Soulier and Fernando notched out a segment of the counter to create a built-in table where the homeowner can sit to read the morning paper and admire his kitchen.

▼ Set in a low counter, the back of the cook top is as accessible as the front. The table-height breakfast booth absorbs little floor area; an adjacent pencil drawer takes advantage of storage space and turns this corner into a kitchen desk center.

GREAT IDEA

Filler Up

Fillers—essentially, drawers turned on end—at junctions between the base cabinets and appliances can be customized with pegboards, racks, rods, and narrow shelves to place kitchen equipment within reach.

Slipped between stove and cabinet, this compartment has been fitted out with magnetic strips to keep knives at hand, a use recommended only for childless homes. Another one, by the sink, holds soap and sponges.

Pullout work surfaces

Low cooktop accessible to seated user

Easy-grip handles

Low counters and cooktop

Low sink with legroom

Open circulation with wheelchair maneuvering space

Single-lever faucet with pullout spray

Front-mounted range controls

Lazy Susan storage

Rollout shelves

Appliance garage

NEVER-FAIL KITCHEN RECIPE

It used to be a given that every kitchen had limitations—hard-to-reach shelves, traffic bottlenecks, unavoidable bending, stooping, straining, and carrying to prepare meals and put things away. Here is a kitchen that proves that assumption wrong. Designed by a team from The Ohio State University and Lowe's, it is a kitchen that sifts out the problems but saves the taste and style.

Designed squarely within the parameters of universal design, the kitchen anticipates the needs of people of different sizes, ages, and physical abilities. Most of the storage is easy to reach—no ceiling-scraping cabinets here—and the appliances are within easy reach of tall, short, seated, and standing users. At 23' by 21'6" (7 x 6.6 m), the L-shaped kitchen is small enough to keep work areas conveniently close, but large enough to incorporate counter space at every workstation. Circulation routes around the kitchen are clear and direct. Wide pathways let people share the kitchen without rubbing shoulders and allow wheelchairs to get around easily.

Good overall lighting makes the room inviting and fully visible. Lights inside cabinets with patterned glass doors help expose the contents and lend panache. Undercabinet lights double as accents and task lights. The resilient cork floor, an environmentally friendly product, reduces fatigue for those on their feet, and provides a firm, smooth, nonslip surface for wheelchairs.

Variable Heights

The designers inserted appliances around the room at points higher and lower than standard, bringing them all to a level that works for the widest range of people. Children and seated users can reach the racks in the raised dish-

washer, for instance, and a tall adult can do so as well without much bending. The oven was installed midwall, equally accessible to seated and standing cooks. Located under the counter in the island, the microwave and stacked refrigerator drawers make a handy snack center that even the kids can use. The side-by-side refrigerator puts the freezer section within general reach, too.

Legroom under the cooktop and the cleanup sink enable seated users to draw close, as do the high, deep toe kicks in the base cabinets. The sink has a single-lever, pullout faucet to simplify cleaning, and a hot water dispenser that takes hot kettles out of the equation when preparing a hot drink. The cooktop is smooth, making it easier to move pots on and off, and the controls are clustered at the front where the cook can reach them (but small children can-

not) without moving around or reaching over burners. Another convenience: a hinged, wall-mounted pot filler adds water to pots at the cooktop, so that lifting and carrying heavy, water-filled pots from the sink is unnecessary.

▶ Rollout shelves were selected with specific contents in mind; a high-sided shelf keeps small appliances from falling out, and a shelf with vertical dividers supports and separates trays, boards, and pans for easy retrieval. The wall oven is 36 inches (91.4 cm) above the floor, where it is comfortable for seated or standing users to reach.

▼ The large, L-shaped island puts a wide swath of counters within reach of every workstation. The food-preparation, cooking, and cleanup areas cluster at the inner corner of the room for convenient access, yet are far enough apart to allow several people to work in the kitchen at once.

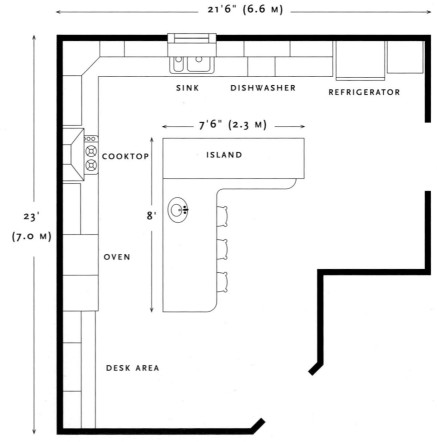

Side-by-side refrigerator

Lower wall oven

Undercounter microwave

Undercounter refrigerator drawers

Rollout shelves

Raised dishwasher

Remote control window covering

Counters at different heights

Lower sink with legroom beneath

Cooktop with legroom beneath

Nonslip cork flooring

Pull-down cabinet

D-shaped cabinet hardware

Single-lever faucet

Lever-style faucets

Rocker-style light switches

Rounded corners on counters

GREAT IDEA

Visual Borders

Spice up your kitchen counters with accent strips that add flavor to the design while identifying countertop edges. The solid-surface counters in this kitchen integrate bands of contrasting color—dark strips in light counters, light strips in dark counters—that complement the design and make the edges easily visible; the rounded-edge profile offers added protection from bumps. Wood, laminate, and tile strips also make smart looking border bands.

Island Paradise

This kitchen has a second sink, especially designed for food preparation. Installed in the table-height counter of the island, it is a great place to sit and chop vegetables. Next to it is a cutting board drawer that adds an extra, sturdy work surface when needed, and has legroom beneath. The 38-inch (96.5 cm)-high counter in the island is a work surface that is easy on the back for people standing.

The cabinet system is full of good ideas. There is the slatted rack conveniently located above the dishwasher, which stores dishes singly instead of in heavy, unwieldy stacks. There are the rimmed pullout shelves that organize trays, small appliances, and cleaning supplies, and bring them into reach. There are deep drawers designed for pots and pans. There is the pull-down unit that lowers shelves from upper cabinets into range for children or seated users.

At the end of the room, the designers reserved space for a desk area. Outfitted with cabinets matching those in the kitchen proper, it's a quiet corner where homeowners can come to catch up on paperwork, out of the center of activity—but close enough to join in the conversation.

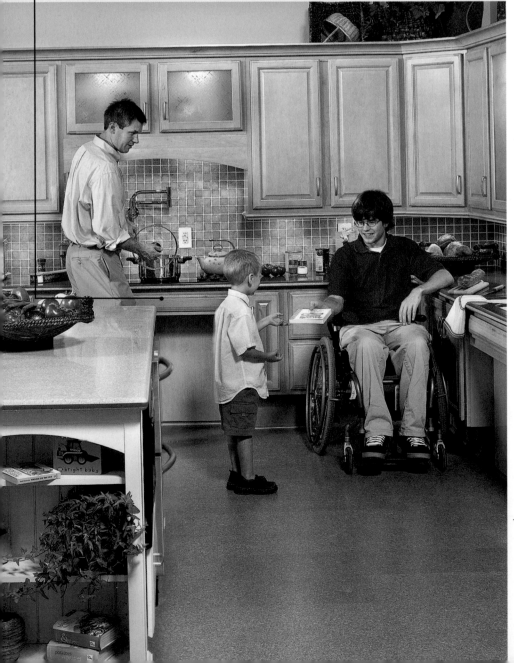

◄ All appliances and sinks are positioned for access by tall, short, and seated users. The efficient island includes a table-height counter and a broad, higher work surface with accessible shelves, microwave, and refrigerated snack drawers underneath.

▼ Counters at different heights and a pullout cutting board suit a variety of uses—and users.

MEASURING UP

For Lori Bentley, of Bentley Design & Remodeling, taking measurements when planning a kitchen means more than running a tape measure around the room. It means measuring the people who will use the space and making sure it will function well for them all.

In this case, Bentley began by noting the height of one homeowner—5 feet, 6 inches (1.65 m)—plus the arm length and chair measurements of the other, a tall man who has used a wheelchair since being injured in a car accident. Calculations in hand, Bentley designed an airy, attractive kitchen that both of them enjoy using.

She began by breaking open the owners' boxy, 11-by-19-foot (3.4 × 5.8 m), 1970s galley kitchen, removing its confining walls to create a large, open family room/kitchen/dining area.

An angled island becomes the heart of the new kitchen. On one side, the island houses an undercounter oven and a cooktop with legroom beneath. A lower, table-height counter on the other side serves as an eating area, food-preparation station, or conversation center. Bentley relied on strategic measurements here too: Calculating a clear path for the cooktop hood to vent through the roof trusses, she identified the most practical location for the island. Then, threading the wiring through the attic, down the outside wall, under the slab and into the island, she placed the hood controls within easy reach under the cooktop.

Clear Passage

The sink, dishwasher, refrigerator, raised undercounter microwave, and pantry line up neatly along the outside wall of the room, conveniently close to the island but reserving wide, open floor space for wheelchair circulation. A generously long countertop work surface streams from refrigerator to sink to wall, with accessible, undercounter cabinets beneath. Deep, 8-inch (20.3 cm)-high toe kick spaces enable wheelchair users to get close to the cabinets.

Counters here and at the cooktop are set 2 inches (5 cm) lower than standard or 34 inches (86.4 cm) above the floor. With surfaces this high, both homeowners can work comfortably—she, standing, and he, seated. The cabinet under the sink features doors that hide legroom area and retract out of the way when opened. Seated here at cleanup time, the homeowner can reach the compact dishwasher drawer on one side, and the pullout trash bin on the other.

Pantry Conversion

Before the remodel, the kitchen had a reach-in pantry that was large enough to soak up valuable floor area but too small for a wheelchair to negotiate well. Bentley did away with that pantry, specifying a slim but highly efficient cabinet that hugs the wall and features drawers and shelving that are equally accessible to all.

Recessed overhead fixtures pour general lighting across the kitchen floor and workstations; pendant lights add task lighting at the island. Undercabinet lights provide closer nonglare lighting for computer work at the kitchen desk. By clustering the kitchen storage under counters and against one corner wall, Bentley reserved room for a broad greenhouse-style window bay over the sink. The glass extends down to countertop level, spreading natural light across both the plants and the work surface and sharing the view with everyone, standing or seated.

GREAT IDEA

Pantry Panels and Drawers

Items stored at the back of cavernous pantry shelves are hard to spot, let alone retrieve.
Rather than deep shelves, try full-extension drawers and shallow, vertical shelving panels.
Some of these commercially available shelves are mounted on cabinet doors that swing wide
on 180-degree hinges for convenient access. Others revolve into view and easy reach, spinning
aside for clear access to shallow shelves on the pantry wall.

Before

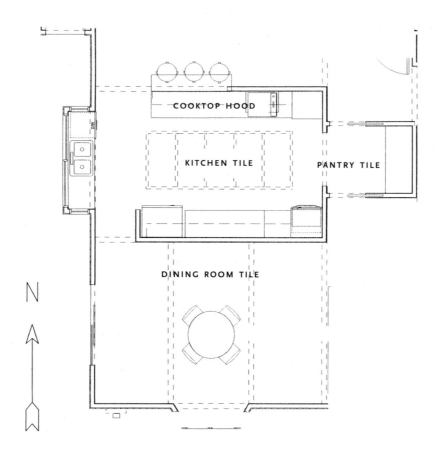

COOKTOP HOOD

KITCHEN TILE

PANTRY TILE

DINING ROOM TILE

N

After

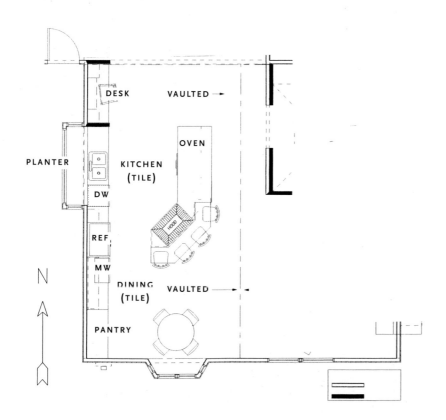

DESK

VAULTED →

OVEN

PLANTER

KITCHEN
(TILE)

DW

HOOD

REF

MW

DINING
(TILE)

VAULTED →

PANTRY

N

▲ Walls around the original kitchen cramped the
circulation area, and the pantry was large but
inaccessible. Bentley removed the walls and
pantry, reorienting the kitchen around a multifunctional island and expanding circulation space
while maintaining an efficient work center.

▼ Bright and spacious, with a handsome, multipurpose island and a big window bay, this kitchen seems designed for looks alone. But every detail, from the wide, smooth-paved floors to under-counter appliances to lower-than-standard counters whose light tone stands out clearly against the cabinets, enables the room to meet the needs of the two homeowners.

Versatile pullout storage

Efficient appliance lineup

Single-lever faucet with pullout spray

Dishwasher drawer

Side-by-side refrigerator/ freezer

Microwave under raised counter for use sitting or standing

Low, shallow sink with legroom underneath

Cooktop with legroom underneath

8-inch (20.3 cm)-high toe kicks under cabinets

Countertops of various heights

Lower window

Accessible outlets

Clear floor space for maneuverability

Easy-grip cabinet pulls

HIDDEN DIFFERENCE

The owner had one request for this kitchen remodel: make it look beautiful, not "different." And that's what designer Heidi Lawrence, AKBD, did.

Her first move was to turn the cramped 1960s kitchen into an open, welcoming area with plenty of circulation space. She did it by removing the wall between the 10-by-11-foot (3 × 3.4 m) kitchen and the living room, connecting the two with an inviting, roundtable peninsula where friends can gather while the host prepares dinner. A palette of environmentally friendly materials—slate-look compressed concrete countertops, reclaimed oak flooring and handsome cabinetry made from cherry grown in a managed forest—unifies the space and satisfies one of the homeowner's other wishes.

Simple door and drawer fronts disguise the fact that the kitchen is chock full of storage, most of it accessible to the homeowner, who uses a wheelchair. The armoirelike unit by the living area, for example, contains undercounter drawers for dishes. There's a pullout shelf under the cooktop for pots and pans, a recessed cabinet under the sink (making that cabinet area functional without compromising legroom), a set of lighted cubby-style shelves over the cooking center, a lazy Susan in the corner, and a sprinkling of countertop drawers. There even are drawers above and below the dishwasher drawer left of the sink.

To the right is the room's command center. The homeowner can chat with friends at the 30-inch (76.2 cm)-high peninsula while popping something into the undercounter microwave or adjusting the lights at the multiswitch panel just above. Lawrence carefully positioned the lights in the angled ceiling to avoid shadows and glare; the beam goes onto the edge of the counter.

The laundry room off the kitchen is so attractive it doesn't need to hide behind a door. The cabinets match those in the kitchen, and the hardy laminate counters look much like the more luxurious concrete. Located by the garage door, the laundry counter makes a good landing place for things carried in from the car.

Shallow sink with legroom for seated user

Lever-handle faucet, pull-down spray

Dishwasher drawer

Undercounter microwave

Oven with side-hinge door

Short, shallow side-by-side refrigerator

Low cooktop with legroom

Front-loaded washer and dryer

Varied counter and work station heights for standing and seated users

Peninsula supported with recycled steel central post to allow legroom

Consolidated, easy-to-reach electrical switches

Open shelves and clear cabinet doors

Balanced lighting

◄ The rhythmic pattern of counter and work center heights, the handsome cabinetry, and the dynamic mix of natural and electric lighting come together in a kitchen that is equally attractive and user friendly. The peninsula table marks the connection point between cooking and living areas; its supporting post leaves unobstructed legroom.

▲ Every cook would appreciate a command center like this, where cleanup area, utensil storage, microwave, and electrical console all are within reach, and close to the kitchen "table." There's legroom under the sink, but not at the exclusion of recessed storage with cherry doors that match the rest of the cabinetry.

SPOTLIGHT

Floor Show

Flooring plays a leading role in the success of home design. Smart flooring choices make it safer and easier to get around in a house, while adding beauty and character that will garner rave reviews.

When it comes to floors, universal design has several goals. The surface should be smooth and even, to avoid tripping hazards and facilitate walking and playing as well as rolling carts, strollers, and wheelchairs. It should be firm but forgiving, able to stand up to the impact of heels, canes, and wheels; yet kind on legs and feet, and able to soften the blow somewhat if a person falls. It should be slip-resistant, nonglare, durable, easy to maintain. Ideally it should offer some sound insulation value. And the pattern or design of the flooring should not only look good but also help with spatial orientation—subtly identifying transition points between spaces and marking room perimeters.

To accomplish all that, the best choices are uncarpeted, hard floors, and low-pile,

tight-weave carpeting. Hard flooring can be wood, vinyl, rubber, laminate, stone, or tile. Select a nonglossy, nonskid finish, such as oil-finish textured wood, matte-surface vinyl, and unpolished stone or tile. Resilient flooring such as vinyl, rubber, and cork is easiest on the legs and a friendlier surface should someone fall. If allergies are a concern, ask for hypoallergenic flooring, finishes, adhesives, and seals, as well as flooring that can be cleaned with allergen-free products.

Tile the Bathroom

Textured or matte-finish ceramic or porcelain tile makes sense especially in the bathroom, because it is water-resistant and easy to wash. Keep the grout lines as thin as possible, to maintain a smooth surface and avoid creating grooves that catch toes, canes, and wheels. The grout itself should be moisture-resistant, too.

Uncarpeted floors are best, but in some parts of the house it's nice to have a warm,

soft, and quiet carpeted surface. Choose tight-weave, high-density carpet with smooth backing and a smooth, untextured pile no more than $\frac{1}{2}$-inch (1.3 cm) high. Make sure it is antibacterial, stain-resistant, and easycare. Attach the carpet firmly to the floor to prevent accident-causing ripples and frayed edges. Throw rugs are real hazards; if you can't resist having one, make it fringeless and attach it securely to the floor. Better yet, design an area "rug" into the flooring itself.

Indeed, floors have considerable design potential. Light-colored flooring helps to brighten dark rooms. Flooring tones that contrast with walls and furnishings clarify the space and its contents. Pattern, tone, and material changes in the floor map the living area, identifying hallways, rooms, and transition points. Decorative borders around room perimeters, kitchen islands, and other built-in elements offer a visual means of orientation, and simply look beautiful.

▶ Different woods—cherry, maple, birch, and bamboo—run in different directions across this smooth floor to organize and distinguish the living areas. The free-form borders add an artful twist.

▼ The "rug" in this entryway is nonskid, easy-care, and a perfect complement to the surrounding flooring. That's because it's made of the same smooth, mop-clean material as the rest of the floor—unpolished stone tiles. Arranged on the diagonal and surrounded by a mosaic border, the tile rug identifies the entry area without introducing the tripping and slipping risks of an actual rug.

Gallery

KITCHEN STORAGE

Universal design takes kitchen storage to a new level—a level where items can be reached effortlessly by all. Undercounter pullouts and lazy Susans replace deep shelves; storage units are close to appliances and counters where their contents will be used; and creative accessories keep items in order and easy to find.

▼ Adjustable racks and varied drawer and shelf sizes accomodate different items keeping them in place and easy to retrieve.

Movable Storage

This little corner is brimming with clever, space-smart storage. The spice rack pulls out to the counter's edge and swivels 360 degrees for access to shelves on all four sides. And morning coffee making is a cinch, thanks to the space-saving swing-up shelf. The coffeemaker remains on the shelf, plugged in, even when the shelf is stowed under the counter behind a cabinet door. In the evening, the owner pulls a lever to bring out the shelf; a spring-loaded hardware system enables him to lift the shelf without exertion. He fills the coffeemaker, sets a timer, and come morning the coffee brews itself.

◄ An inch (2.5 cm) or so of space at the end of an island or counter is enough for a handy recessed knife rack in a kitchen where children won't roam. Held with a magnetic strip and protected behind a perforated metal screen, the knives can be arranged in any way. A strip of electrical outlets adds value to the storage panel.

Gallery

SEATING

Everyone appreciates a place to sit down in the kitchen, whether to take the back strain and foot fatigue out of meal preparation, to accommodate a wheelchair, or simply to relax and socialize.

▶ A drop-leaf panel creates a seating place in this very traditional kitchen. The sturdy supporting posts do not block legroom when extended and recede neatly into the island when not in use.

▶ Pull this 30-inch (76.2 cm)-high table from its 30-inch (76.2 cm)-deep drawer opening in the island, fold down the hinged front and side panels, and you've got a good-size dining table. Mounted on heavy duty, full-extension drawer hardware, the cantilevered table has no legs to block seating; when closed, it looks like a standard cabinet.

◄ To create legroom for a seated user, a cart rolls out from under this cooktop. Parked by the cook top, it keeps pots and pans close, and furnishes a handy work surface. The back of the cart matches the kitchen cabinetry, so it blends in.

GREAT IDEA

Half a Cabinet

A slender base cabinet in this kitchen island supports an overhanging counter for stool seating. With a wink and a smile, the contractor turned the slim cabinet into a fun space where a small child can play near the action but out from under foot. The same concept works for cabinet openings designed to provide legroom for seated users.

PRODUCTS FOR THE KITCHEN

▼ Large enough to hold six place settings, these dishwasher drawers can be stacked or placed on each side of the sink for convenient access from a sitting or standing position. The handles are easy to grip and the push-button controls, with a child-lock option, are simple to use. The units have energy and water-saving capabilities.

▼ Organize and secure dishes in a drawer that has a pegboard base and shaped posts. The durable beech posts can be rearranged as needed; fastening nuts hold them solidly in place.

▲ Corner storage space is neither wasted nor inaccessible here, where undercounter drawers of varied depths and with different inserts arrange kitchen utensils and equipment. The deep drawers ride on full-extension glides to bring all contents into view and easy reach.

◄ Spice jars stay organized, visible, and at hand in an undercounter storage system. The modules that rest on this pullout surface can be lifted by the side handles and carried to the food-prep station.

▶ Use a stainless steel cabinet insert to pivot upper shelves into reach for short or seated people. The hardware fits a range of cabinet widths; your contractor supplies the box-style shelves.

▼ Drawers keep the trash bin handy but out of the way. Heavy-duty full-extension slides bring the bin into the open, along with supplies that can be stored in the wire rack. Other models accommodate two bins for trash sorting. Attach a cabinet front to match the others in the room.

▲ No heavy lifting is required here: Hardware attached to the base cabinet shelf lifts the shelf and mixer to counter height. The hardware works with any size shelf and holds up to 60 pounds (27.2 kg).

▲ Designed for you to cover with a panel that matches your cabinetry, this dishwasher drawer blends in so well that it can be installed wherever it is most convenient—perhaps under the counter in a wet bar or near the dining room.

▼ Squatting down and groping into the depth of a low cabinet isn't necessary if you have tray-style drawers. Strong enough to hold bowls, pans, and other large items, these sturdy units bring items into view and easy reach, while the surrounding lip keeps things from falling out.

▼ Otherwise wasted spaces between base cabinets and appliances can be put to use as convenient storage centers by the sink, stove, or food-prep area. Keep cooking utensils, small pans, dish brushes, and towels on washable, perforated steel panels, or stow spices and bottles on slim shelves.

▲ Nothing gets lost in the far reaches of this corner cabinet. When the door is opened, the front shelves emerge and move to the side, allowing the recessed corner shelves to be pulled out next to the others for full access. Wire edges protect shelf contents without reducing visibility. The mechanism fits both left and right corners.

▲ Install a microwave oven under the counter where it can be used conveniently by children and seated adults as well as the rest of the family. This built-in microwave, which can be installed in cabinet openings of several different sizes, has a door that drops down for access from both sides and a sleek, easy-grip handle.

◀ Along with dishwasher drawers, warming drawers, and other appliances, this coordinated suite includes an unobtrusive, counter-depth, side-by-side refrigerator/freezer and an under-counter refrigerator for wines and other beverages. Rounded handles have no sharp corners and are comfortable to grip.

▼ Not only does this pantry glide out of the cabinet, but it also swings on its base for a clear approach to the shelves. The unit can be customized with shelves of different sizes.

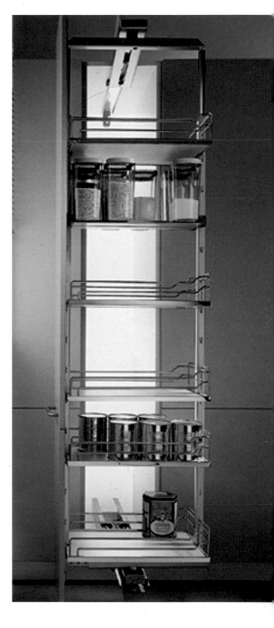

▲ A long undercounter pullout at the right height for a seated user becomes a table or a handy workspace. When stowed behind the drawer front, the sturdy, space-efficient surface keeps passageways clear.

◀ Crafted specifically for universal design, this standard cabinet line includes cooktop and sink bases with legroom, a raised base for the dishwasher, and low base cabinets with a tall, deep toe kick.

◄ Operating like a drawer, this full-extension, undercounter unit brings the shelves into the room so that pantry items can be retrieved without reaching or stretching.

▼ These large-capacity shelves swing into the open for full access to all items, even those stowed deep within the cabinet. The shelves have a protective rail and a nonslip surface and are adjustable in height.

▲ Stacked drawers place generous freezer space within comfortable reach wherever access to frozen foods in needed. Offered in several styles, they feature bright interior lighting and an alarm to alert you if a drawer is left open.

▲ Custom configured and built to fit your needs and equipment, full-extension glide-out storage units can be designed as shelves for pots, bowls, and storage bins; as shallow trays for spices and utensils; and as drawers with vertical dividers to keep platters, cookie sheets, and cutting boards organized and at hand.

▼ Tuck this compact icemaker under the counter to bring ice into arm's reach. It can be installed anywhere, since it requires no drain. The machine comes in several door finishes, including stainless steel with a sleek, accessible handle, or can be fitted with a custom panel to match surrounding cabinetry.

▼ Tailor the kitchen to your family's needs with a height-adjustable cooktop, work surface, or sink that moves with the touch of a button from 28 to 36 inches (71.1 to 91.4 cm) high. The mechanism is the same for all three uses and is available for your contractor to install on counters 36 to 48 inches (91.4 to 120 cm) wide.

◀ With a tall, deep toe kick space and 32¹/₂-inch (82.6 cm)-high countertop, this cabinet line is comfortable for a user who is seated or in a wheelchair. The drawer in this unit is high enough to be reached with ease, and the tambour door opens without intruding into the circulation area.

▼ The door of this electric convection wall oven opens to the side a full 180 degrees to provide clear access from the front. The rod-style handle is within reach for standing or seated users, and the control knobs can be turned without exertion.

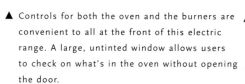

▲ Controls for both the oven and the burners are convenient to all at the front of this electric range. A large, untinted window allows users to check on what's in the oven without opening the door.

▲ Press a button to lower the base of this wall oven into reach for short or seated users and for transfer of food without lifting. The rest of the time, the counter space underneath is clear for other uses. The convection oven can hold wire racks, baking, and broiling trays, and retains heat by opening from the bottom.

▼ Mix and match components in this modular system to enable countertop cooking. The combo here includes a griddle, fryer, and cool-to-the-touch induction cooktop with a wok attachment. You can run the units length or widthwise; and place the controls in a group or separated, to the front, side, or elsewhere. Clear the space under the cooktop and fryer to make legroom for a seated user.

▲ A pullout, undercounter rack for dinnerware solves three problems: Dishes and glassware are convenient to reach and put away; there are no heavy stacks of dishes to hoist; and each piece is protected from chipping in a separate, epoxy-coated wire slot.

▶ The standard model of this dishwasher can be installed under a low, 34-inch (86.4 cm)-high counter without modifications. The controls are easy-to-use pictorial pushbuttons; users can set the machine to remember the last program selected, so it can simply be repeated. Choose one of several door styles, or install your own panel to match your cabinetry.

SMART BATHROOMS

Nowhere does universal design yield more beautiful results than in the bathroom. That's because ample circulation space, smart organization, convenience, and other universal design essentials are signatures of good overall bathroom design, too. And it's because so many dazzling products are available that satisfy both universal design needs and stylish tastes.

Even compact universal design bathrooms tend to feel airy, because the space is open and there's elbowroom between appliances. In fact, the rooms do need to be at least a little larger than the once-standard 5-by-7-foot (1.5 × 2.1 m) cubicle so they can accommodate a central 5-foot (1.5 m)-diameter area for circulation and wheelchair maneuverability. Pocket doors and out-swinging doors preserve precious space in a small room.

Shower Easy

No-curb or low-curb showers are a design highlight in bathrooms today, and they're a natural for universal design baths. Extending seamlessly from the bathroom floor, these elegant shower zones with floors slightly sloped to the drain present no tripping obstacles, and can be entered on wheels. A built-in bench or folding seat, a handheld shower spray on a vertical slide bar, integrated soap compartments, and strategically placed grab bars make the shower a sumptuous, safe washing place. Here, as elsewhere in the bathroom, pressure-balancing valves keep hot water temperatures safe, and nonskid flooring prevents slips.

If there's room, many homeowners add a bathtub as well. Dropped into a surround that features a seating or transition area, with side-mounted controls reachable from outside or inside the tub, it's a perfect place for parents to bathe the kids or adults to bathe in luxury.

▶ The angle of the counter and the cabinet tower between the twin-sink vanity and sit-down dressing table marks a boundary while maximizing open floor space. Floating the tub in a large surround establishes generous seating platforms at each end. Large, frosted glass windows and well-placed fixtures permeate the room with light.

For the Sake of Vanity

Vanities and sinks offer countless opportunities for customization to maximize comfort, convenience and accessibility. Choose vanity heights to fit the users—higher to minimize bending for someone with a bad back or lower for children or seated users. A low vanity section can serve as a dressing table for now, and with behind-the-wall pipes in place and a countertop section that can be cut or replaced, it's easy to drop in a sink later. A large mirror that runs from the countertop to the ceiling works for everyone. Adjustable mirrors add versatility.

Flank each wash station with undercounter drawers, preferably fitted with easy-grip, C-shape handles. Keep the area under the low sink open, or furnish it with a cabinet whose door could be removed to create legroom. Shield any exposed pipes to prevent burns.

Sinks can be embedded in the countertop, overhang the edge, perch on top like a bowl, or stand alone, with or without an integrated counter area. For convenient use, select one that is set toward the front of the counter, ideally with a rear drain so the pipes can be positioned against the wall or even behind it. Place faucets where they are accessible for children or seated users—for example, at the side of the sink. Lever handles are good, as are single-control faucets with a pullout hose.

Towels at Hand

Stow towels and bathroom supplies within arm's reach of where they will be used—that is, by the shower, tub and vanity. Sturdy towel bars or a few shelves tucked between wall studs or mounted on the wall will do the job. Remember to leave space between wall-mounted units and the floor to provide toe room for wheelchair users.

It's important to install grab bars around the room—in the shower, by the toilet and tub, wherever a holding-on place may be needed—but think of them as stylish accessories as well as safety features. Grab bars today come in beautiful finishes, colors, and designs, often matching the other bathroom hardware. Even if you don't want to install all the grab bars at this point, put in the blocking for them while the walls are open; it will save money later.

Plan the electrical components of the bathroom with an eye toward convenience and practicality. Include ambient lighting as well as task lighting at the shower and vanity. Place some electrical outlets above the vanity, and consider an appliance drawer. Add a phone jack near the tub or toilet. Locate light switches where they'll be needed around the room and outside the bathroom door; lighted rocker switches can double as nightlights. Radiant floor heating is a nice option to keep the room cozy.

▼ The glass counter, vessel sink, and wall-mounted faucet are a chic ensemble for a powder room or small bath. The space-efficient combo features undercounter legroom and handsome, easy-grip faucet handles.

Chair-Height Toilets

The typical chair seat is about 17 or 18 inches (43.2 or 45.7 cm) off the ground, a comfortable height for most people. Toilets are available with chair-height seats, too. They're just 2 or 3 inches (5.1 or 7.6 cm) taller than standard, but easier on the knees and better for wheelchair users. Manufacturers offer chair-height toilets in a wide range of styles, such as this one from Kohler.

◀ Open baths such as this stylish, organic room lend themselves well to universal design. With no door or threshold, the shower is barrier free. The concrete bench is hydronically heated for comfort, and the vanity is suspended at a height suitable for seated or standing users. Blocking behind the walls is ready for grab bar installation. Wraparound windows bring in natural light, and ambient light reflects off the ceiling for balanced illumination.

NEW-ANGLED DESIGN

The master suite in this house had plenty of space; it just was in the wrong place. The bedroom hogged most of the square footage, putting the squeeze on the closets and bathroom. Architect Linda Randolph reshuffled the plan, making room for two spacious walk-in closets and a large, gracious bathroom that the owners can enjoy, even when one owner's Parkinson's disease occasionally confines her to a walker or wheelchair.

The accessible new bathroom feels larger and more dynamic than the 12-by-13-foot (3.7 ¥ 4 m) space it occupies. That's because Randolph used angles to segment the room into zones and lengthen walls. An angled wall for the twin-sink vanity reaches away from the entry, clearing a large, central circulation circle. Parallel to the vanity is a tub surround that, thanks to its angular orientation, has room for the tub and a large seating area.

Another angled wall radiates away from the entry in the other direction, this one a wall for the toilet room. Both the long, angled wall and another, shorter wall in the curbless shower contain glass block windows that provide natural light for the fully interior toilet compartment.

Adjacent to the vanities, Randolph placed a well-lighted dressing table with undercounter legroom. The cabinet under the sink can be removed to create legroom here as well; the sink plumbing has been set to the rear. Cabinet towers convenient to the vanity and tub store toiletries and towels. Though close to the tub, the vanity mirrors are heated to resist steam buildup. Radiant heating in high-use areas keeps the nonskid tile floors comfortable, and helps dry them.

Wet Area

The jet-fitted tub features integral handholds and offers users a choice of a fixed or pullout spray. Randolph replaced the old sunken tub with a shower, reusing the dropped tub pan to form a curbless shower floor. Randolph used an extension of the toilet room wall plane to mold a deep, chair-height bench within easy reach of the handheld spray.

With its angled wall, the toilet compartment is quite roomy, large enough for a pedestal sink and a chair-height toilet with enough space beside for wheelchair transfer. Grab bars—and towel bars that meet grab bar specifications—are peppered around the bathroom, in the shower, at the shower entry, in the tub area, and the toilet room. Blocking installed behind the walls will simplify the task of adding more bars if wanted.

Continuing the theme of angles, recessed can lights radiate across the bathroom ceiling. Running the fixtures on angled paths, Randolph supplied good lighting to every zone of the room.

▶ Small mosaic tiles make a nonskid "carpet" in the curbless shower. A tiled wall extension forms a comfortably deep bench seat in the shower.

GREAT IDEA

Patterns in Tile

Like chain-link necklaces, bands of tile accent strips wrap around this bathroom, dressing up the space. They have a more pragmatic purpose as well, forming a subtle, attractive visual guide that outlines the shower platform and signals the junctions of floor and wall, wall and tub deck.

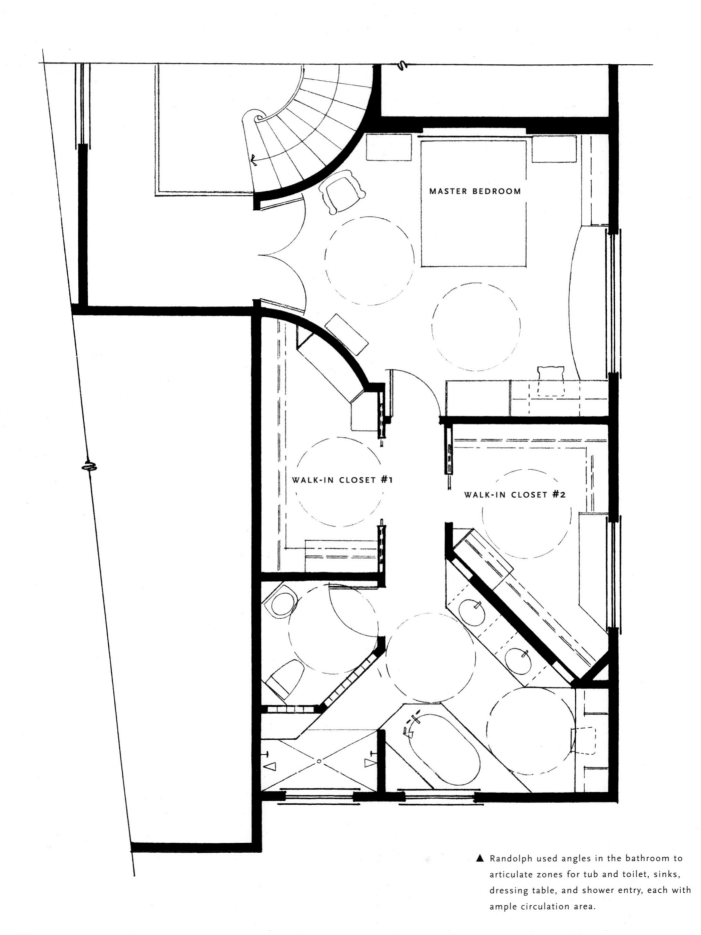

MASTER BEDROOM

WALK-IN CLOSET #1

WALK-IN CLOSET #2

▲ Randolph used angles in the bathroom to
articulate zones for tub and toilet, sinks,
dressing table, and shower entry, each with
ample circulation area.

▼ Angled at the ends to ensure clear passage, the vanity has removable cabinetry under one sink to provide legroom for a seated user. Heated, steam-free mirrors across the vanity and on the opposite wall expand the space and spread the light.

Curbless shower

Handheld sprays

Tub seating/ transfer area

Accessible tub faucets

Chair-height toilet

Lever handles

Grab bars

Nonskid flooring

Balanced lighting

Wide, low-threshold entry

Vanity with legroom for seated user

5-foot (1.5 m) turning radius

Visual clues in finishes

Rocker light switches

FITS-ALL BATH

Small children, tall people, vision impaired or hard of hearing, wheelchair users and those with arthritis... it doesn't matter. Here's a bathroom that's a good fit for all—and that sparkles with personality of its own. Accessibility expert Cynthia Leibrock, of agingbeautifully.org, and architect Mary Beth Rampolla, of Design Collaboratives, designed it for Kohler to demonstrate how accommodating and good-looking universal design bathrooms can be.

The twin-sink vanity can be adjusted and rearranged at any time. The side-by-side countertops, installed on wall tracks, can be aligned to make one long vanity top or positioned from 25 to 42 inches (63.5 to 106.7 cm) above the floor for different users. The vanity cabinets are really carts on casters; they can be spaced to accommodate seated users or moved to provide storage and counter space elsewhere in the room.

A simple, textured chrome rod placed across each vanity functions as a nonslip grab bar, convenient towel bar, and visual cue identifying the counter edge. The solid surface counters are hypoallergenic; Leibrock chose a light color for them to contrast with the wall and help spread reflected light from overhead fixtures. High-arch faucets assure clear access to the sinks. Their aerated sprays are quieter than high-pressure sprays—appreciated by people who have trouble distinguishing words when there is background noise. The faucets sport graceful, paddle-style faucet levers with red and blue coding for hot and cold.

Safety and Privacy

Matte-finish, mosaic ceramic tiles in a meshwork of grout lines make the floor slip-resistant. Slim dividing walls afford privacy for the commode and bathing area. They also catch steam and spray from the shower, which keeps the vanity floor dry and the mirrors clear. Bands of chrome, punctuated by vertical shafts, wrap around the tub, shower, and commode spaces, lending a clean, modern aesthetic as well as uninterrupted grab bar support.

Polished-finish wall tiles that simply wipe clean contrast with the floor color to help mark floor edges. Likewise, the dark tub and commode are easy to see. The toilet is chair height, elongated to align with a shower wheelchair, and designed for quiet water flow. It shares open space with a contemporary shower post featuring a spray that can be handheld when using the toilet as a chair or attached to a slide bar for showering from a standing position.

The bottom of the bathtub is slip-resistant and flat in contour to minimize falls. Grab bars are arranged at both 9 inches (22.9 cm) above the tub and 34 inches (86.4 cm) above the floor to help a variety of users get in and out. A second handheld shower by the tub is a handy spray at the kids' bath time, and even for seated users outside the bath. Linen closets behind the tub and shower keep towels nearby.

GREAT IDEA

Central Shower Post

Designing a shower for a variety of users can be challenging. This stylish, tiled shower post keeps the handheld spray and controls in easy reach for all, and features easy-to-use, one-lever hardware. Because it is in a corner, it is accessible from several directions.

Curbless shower

Handheld sprays

Pressure-balanced fittings

Removable, under-counter cabinets

C-shape hardware

Grab bars

Elongated toilet

Flat-bottom, slip-resistant bathtub

Lever faucets

Quiet faucets

Adjustable height vanities

Hypoallergenic, solid surface vanity top

▲ Despite its clean lines and soothing color scheme, this bathroom is hard-working, with the user-friendly tub, shower, and commode well-supported by grab bars, and color cues to mark walls, fixtures, and countertops.

▶ Adjustable vanities with shallow, accessible vessel bowls and flexible, rear-mounted pipes can be locked in at the same height or positioned individually for short, tall, or seated users. Cabinets on locking casters can be used as vanity storage or moved to wherever they are needed.

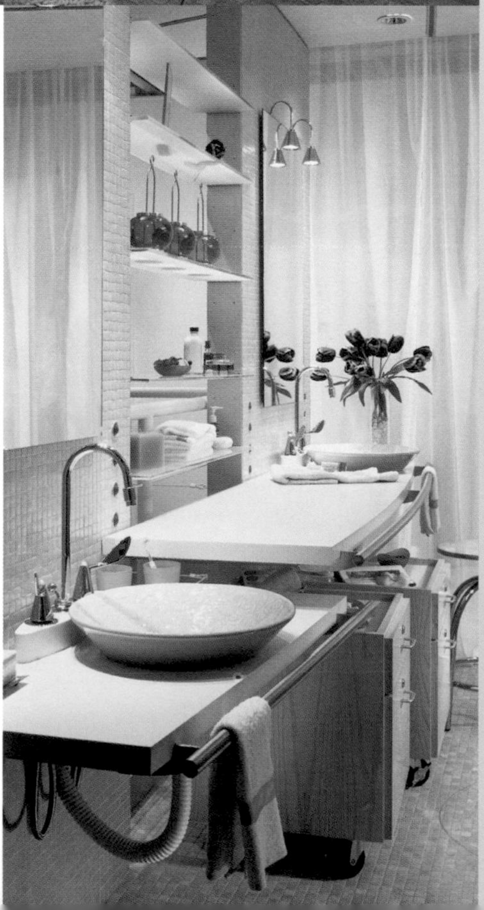

PLEASING COLORS

Accustomed to living in an old, two-story house, the ground-level master suite addition came as a refreshing change for these home-owners. It's not that they disliked the old house—they loved the place. Anticipating health challenges as they grew older, they simply wanted to be ready.

With its handsome frosted glass, curbless shower, and colorful accents, the master bath-room is a perfect blend of fresh aesthetics and subtle accessibility. Design-builder Thomas Buckborough & Associates cleverly allocated space in the 12-by-12-foot (3.7 × 3.7 m) room, tucking the neoangle shower and tub into adjacent corners to preserve a large open area for circulation in the room. The corner space makes the shower deep enough for wheelchair maneuverability, and the tub surround crosses into the shower enclosure to function as a bench. Grab bars are placed at various heights, ready for standing or seated users as they move around in the shower.

Green Light

The fluid green frosted-glass shower panels allow privacy without blocking light. Stopping the shower walls below ceiling height allows sunlight from the room's large, central skylight to penetrate the shower. The tub enjoys natural light from both its skylight and windows. Fixtures dotted around the ceiling provide balanced ambient lighting that radiates down and reflects off the white walls.

Green tile on the tub deck discreetly identifies the seating-transfer surface. White tile below the deck and on surrounding walls contrasts with the floor tile, visually marking boundaries. Decorative accent tiles just below the top of the commode privacy wall help identify the flat, supporting surface. Grab bars by the commode provide additional handholds.

Buckborough chose matte-finish, mosaic tiles to craft a nonskid floor. Color striations assist with the perception of depth along the floor. Radiant heating keeps the floor pleasingly warm.

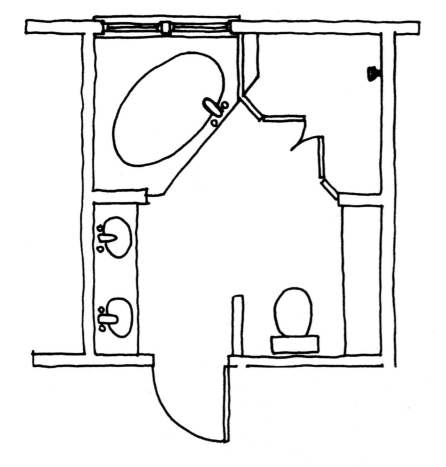

◀ Angling the tub and shower into corners gives them ample space without sacrificing central floor area. The vanity by the tub has wide maneuvering space, too.

▶ The white and green features and the splash of decorative tiles do more than beautify the room; they help organize the space and provide visual cues.

GREAT IDEA

Saloon Doors

Doorless showers aren't for everyone. These homeowners preferred to close the shower for privacy, but a door spanning the wide, accessible shower entry would have cut too deeply into the room's circulation space. Instead, Buckborough installed double doors on double-action "saloon door" hinges. Half the width of a single door, they pivot aside without blocking space inside or outside the shower.

Clear floor space for maneuverability

Curbless shower

Tub surround with transfer space

Offset, accessible tub faucet

Grab bars

Lever and D-shape handles

Handheld shower spray

Nonskid floor

Remote control window covering

Generous lighting

Visual cues for orientation

PEACEFUL RETREAT

The master bedroom and bath are on the second floor of this house, and the homeowners wanted to keep it that way. No problem: Designer Genie Nowicki, of Harrell Remodeling, installed an elevator to ensure effortless second-floor access. But that left only a small powder room on the first floor. To accommodate guests, the owners asked Nowicki to convert the powder room to a larger, fully accessible bathroom. She went further, sculpting a serene bathing space that has become a relaxing retreat for the homeowners themselves.

At 6 ½ by 8 ½ feet (2 × 2.6 m), the new bathroom is not especially large, but the open plan, pocket-style entry door, spare furnishings, and cool, consistent color scheme make it feel spacious. Essentially one rectangular area with a curbless, open shower at the far end, the room has a 5-foot (1.5 m) turning radius to accommodate a wheelchair at the center, offering convenient access to sink, commode, and cabinet. All three of these fixtures are wall mounted, for closer wheelchair access and a sleek, uncluttered look.

The stylish, space-saving sink is mounted 30 inches (76.2 cm) above the floor, where it suits a variety of users, including those in a chair. The towel bars, ordered as accessories to the sink, keep towels at hand yet neatly tucked away under the counter. The storage unit suspended 12 inches (.3 m) above the floor on the opposite wall consolidates linens and toiletries in one place, within easy-to-open, C-handled cabinets and drawers. And the commode is positioned at 18 inches (.5 m) above the floor, or chair height. The tank hides in the wall, which has 2-by-6-inch (5.1 × 15.2 cm) framing instead of the standard 2- by -4 inches (5.1 × 10.2 cm); an unobtrusive panel above the commode contains a push-button flush mechanism and a tank access cover.

Polished marble surrounds the shower and extends around the room as a low-maintenance backsplash and wainscoating. Matte-finish porcelain tiles make a slip-resistant floor, and thin grout lines simplify cleaning. A dam under the floor at the doorway ensures that water from the bathroom will not run onto the adjacent wood floors.

Daylight floods into the room from the shower window and a large, central skylight in the vaulted bathroom ceiling. Track fixtures and recessed cans run across the ceiling and into the skylight tower to permeate all corners of the room with light.

▶ The wall-mounted cabinet consolidates linens and toiletries in a convenient, central place next to the shower and facing the sink. A glass panel with a gracefully rounded corner shields the cabinet from shower spray.

▼ Essentially a "wet room," the bathroom and shower compose one continuous space. The entire floor, covered with slip-resistant matte-finish porcelain tiles, slopes ever so gently to the shower drain.

GREAT IDEA

Integrated Shower Hooks

People with glass showers can have shower hooks. When she ordered the custom panel for the shower, Nowicki had a robe hook integrated into the glass. Lower hooks—inside the shower for a washcloth and outside for a towel—could be integrated just as easily.

Wall-hung sink, commode, and cabinet

Overhanging sink bowl with integrated counter for seated user

Accessible towel rods

Doorless, curbless shower

Single-lever sink faucet

Large mirror positioned for seated or standing user

Slip-resistant tile floor

Low-maintenance wallcovering

Grab bars

Handheld shower spray

C-shaped cabinet handles

Wide-entry pocket door

TALL ORDER

When they asked remodeler Abbie Sladick to remodel the master bathroom in their newly purchased house, the middle-aged couple delivered a tall order. Make the dingy room bright and beautiful, they said. Size it more appropriately for their tall stature. And subtly, elegantly prepare the room to accommodate older relatives who visit as well as their own changing needs in coming years, because they did not want to move again.

Though large, the original bathroom had many of the limitations of a typical bathroom—a tub with no seating deck; a 30-inch (76.2 cm) vanity height; a dark shower stall with entry step (in this case a step down); skimpy, inconvenient storage; and persistent dampness. By removing a couple of large planters that trapped dust and moisture, Sladick, of Abbie Joan Enterprises, cleared the air and also cleared space for handy linen cabinets alongside the bathtub. Exhaust fans on timers dispel moisture after the shower or tub is used.

Vanities with easy-grip linear hardware match the linen cabinets and are extra tall, bringing the vessel sinks up to 36 inches (.9 m). A 10-inch (25.4 cm)-deep tub surround forms a seating platform and a mounting surface for the accessible handheld faucet. Recessed can lights and a window with a remote control shade fill the tub niche with light. The white tub stands out clearly in the stone-clad tub surround, which complements the walls and the nonskid, textured floor tiles in the room.

Breaking Down the Walls

To bring light and a sense of expansiveness to the corner shower, Sladick replaced the shower door with a 32-inch (81.3 cm)-wide, doorless entry and changed the solid entry walls to half walls topped by glass panels. She raised the shower base to create a curbless, no-step entry, sloping the shower floor slightly to the drain. Smaller, matte finish stone tiles and their web of grout lines make a slip-resistant shower floor.

Even with the built-in bench, the shower enclosure incorporates a wide roll-in area for a wheelchair. Controls for the fixed showerhead are by the shower entry for access from outside. Stylish grab bars and a handheld shower spray are close to the bench for a seated user. Grab bars that double as towel bars equip the commode area. Rocker light switches there feature integral lighting so they are easy to locate.

The homeowners are pleased with the remodeled bathroom, and with the knowledge that it will serve them well as they get older. But they aren't the room's only fans. For their young son, washing up in that cool shower is a special treat.

GREAT IDEA

Heat Pump for Constant Water Temp

Tub water too hot? Cools off too quickly? Not here. Sladick embedded a recirculating heat pump in the tub surround. The thermostatically controlled unit keeps the tub water at a constant, safe, cozy temperature and saves on water heating bills to boot. —————

▼ The tall homeowners find their 36-inch (91.4 cm)-high vessel sinks more comfortable to use than lower, standard-height bathroom sinks. A rounded corner and bull nose strips soften the edges of the stone tile tub deck.

Large curbless shower

Shower seat

Tub with seating/transfer platform

In-line tub heater with thermostatic control

Grab bars

Custom-height vanity

Nonskid stone floor tiles

Remote control window covering

Easy-grip hardware

Fixed and handheld shower sprays

Illuminated rocker light switches

Ample lighting

Accessible storage

▼ Glass half walls, a wide entry, and a central light in a domed ceiling turn the formerly claustrophobic shower into a bright, accessible area. Grab bars and an adjustable handheld shower spray are located by the built-in seat.

Gallery

BATHROOM SINKS AND VANITIES

Almost any style of vanity or sink can be used in a universal design bathroom, often right off the shelf or with a few simple adjustments to make it comfortable for a variety of users, including children and seated adults. These examples show how wide the choices are for small and large, traditional and contemporary bathrooms.

▼ Designed to fit the homeowners, this bathroom vanity is at custom heights—a 36-inch (91.4 cm)-high side for a tall person and a 30-inch (76.2 cm)-high side for a person 17 inches (43.2 cm) shorter. Each section has a full complement of storage and counter area, plus handy front-mounted outlets; the cabinet under the low sink has open space for legroom. Windows over the vanity and tub bring in fresh air—a special asset for one of these homeowners, who has chemical sensitivities.

▶ An overhanging sink and a slim vanity are a space-saving combination in this small Craftsman-style master bathroom. The sink overhang creates some legroom for seated users, while the compact cabinetry extends only 12 inches (.3 m) into the room. (The trap hides behind a wall panel that could be removed to allow even more legroom for a wheelchair user.) Custom designed for the space, the mahogany cabinet incorporates both drawers and convenient open shelving. The vanity and granite counter taper toward the wall to keep the entryway clear. The mirror angles up or down as needed.

▶ This ingenious vanity has a secret. The angled base panel adds not only style but also legroom for a seated user. The baffled panel acts as a shield for hot pipes and, attached with a piano hinge, opens to provide access to stored supplies and the sink plumbing. A front-mounted towel bar on one side and medicine cabinet on the other complete the practical, uncluttered setup.

GREAT IDEA

Custom-Cut Bathroom Counter

A granite slab—or, for that matter, any cuttable solid surface—can be shaped into an artistic, one-of-a-kind, accessible bathroom counter. This wavy-edged granite top is designed to fit the space in a powder room and is installed at a 36-inch (.9 m) height to fit the tall homeowner; set a few inches lower, the floating counter would be fine for a seated user. In a solid top, the sink can be popped into place wherever it would be most handy. Here, the undermount sink is off-center in the granite but nicely centered in the small room.

Gallery

BATHROOM STORAGE

A standout feature in well-planned bathrooms is convenient storage—cabinets, shelves, and cubbies that are easy to reach, easy to open, and located close to where their contents will be needed. One of the luxuries of universal design bathrooms is that the storage can be positioned with the convenience of specific users—tall, short, or seated—in mind.

▲
◄ Tucking the vanity and bathroom storage into a corner brings everything into reach from one position. This well-stocked system features below-counter cabinets with slim nonobstructing doors; ample above-counter shelves and drawers of varying depths; a roomy hair dryer garage with a smooth-gliding rolltop door; an upper cabinet whose door won't bump anyone's head when opened; and a glass-doored cabinet with in-cabinet lighting to bring things into view.

GREAT IDEA

Towel Warming Drawer

What could be better than a drawer that keeps a stash of towels by the shower? A drawer that warms them up. This low, easy-access drawer puts to use otherwise empty space under the shower bench. The facing matches the other bathroom cabinetry in the room, but the unit is actually a warming drawer, ordinarily installed in kitchens.

▶ Notching back the upper cabinet frees up counter space and assures that the cabinet door won't hit the head of a child or seated person when it swings open. A shelf in the recessed area puts that storage space to good use here. The undercounter cabinet doors open toward the sink for easiest access.

Gallery

GRAB BARS

Think through how you will move around in the bathroom—getting into the tub, taking a shower, approaching the commode or vanity—and map out where to place grab bars accordingly. Bars that complement the design of the room become accents as well as aids. Angled and horizontal bars are best. When not needed for support, horizontal bars can be used as towel rods.

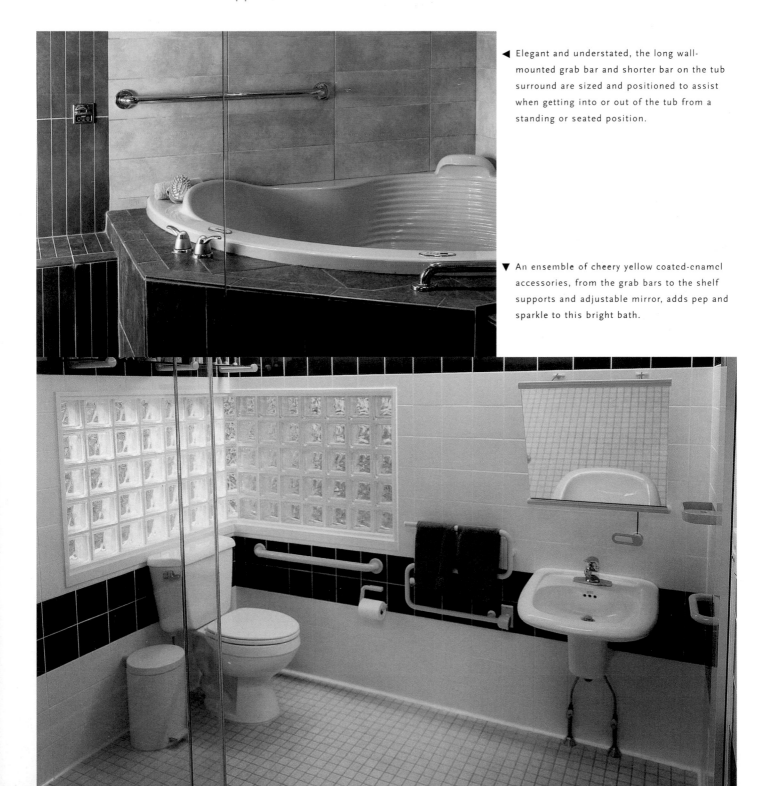

◀ Elegant and understated, the long wall-mounted grab bar and shorter bar on the tub surround are sized and positioned to assist when getting into or out of the tub from a standing or seated position.

▼ An ensemble of cheery yellow coated-enamel accessories, from the grab bars to the shelf supports and adjustable mirror, adds pep and sparkle to this bright bath.

Gallery

TUBS

Make a bathtub—even that old model you've had for years—stylish and user friendly by enclosing it in a surround that is deep enough to provide a surface for seating and maneuvering in and out of the tub. Finish it with materials that complement the room design and set the faucet controls at one end, where they will be accessible but not in the way.

▶ The broad, flat surface of the surround makes a comfortable seat for transfer into this tub. The lever-style faucets and pullout spray are convenient from outside or inside the tub, and offset enough to provide plenty of room for a parent to sit while bathing a child. Paired ceiling fixtures light the tub niche evenly.

▶ Like a ship at sea, this white tub and deck and light-toned wood surround stand out clearly from the deep blue floor and wall. The generous-size surround features seating space at both ends, and a cubby for slippers or towels. The offset faucet handles are accessible from outside the tub; the faucet itself is out of the way against the wall.

Gallery

SHOWERS

Describe a shower that is in the mainstream of contemporary bathroom design—a roomy, well-appointed, stepless extension of the bathroom featuring seating, versatile sprays, and a clear door or no door at all—and you've described a universal design shower as well. A wide entry and spacious interior make a shower both luxurious and accessible.

◄ The finest materials have been molded for practical use in this shower, where a sculptural shower bench of granite and tile offers a wide seating platform at the entrance without crowding the shower space. Niches cut into the stone-tiled walls keep shampoo and soap within reach.

▼ By recessing the framing under the shower floor, the home builder created an economical curbless shower. With nonskid ceramic floor tile, a folding bench, and a handheld spray, the shower works for a variety of users. In a remodeled bathroom, a similar shower could be slipped into the space vacated by a tub; to gain floor area for wheelchair maneuverability, it could share common space outside the shower curtain.

GREAT IDEA

One Door, Two Spaces

Rather than overwhelm the bathroom with doors, the architect designed a "two-fer"— a single, wide door mounted on a 180-degree hinge. When it's pulled in one direction, it encloses the curbless shower; pulled in the other, it encloses the water closet. The frosted glass door and overhead transoms admit light to both spaces.

▼ Riding in an overhead track, this shower door glides open easily and absorbs no floor space; the louvers supply both privacy and ventilation. Designed as a component of a healthy, chemical-free living area, the shower has a nontoxic, polished wall finish and solvent-free, water-based finish and stain on the door.

▲ The extra-wide rain showerhead in this shower assures gentle, overall water coverage. The adjacent track-mounted head is adjustable and detachable, to be used as a supplemental water source or as a handheld.

SPOTLIGHT

Seeing the Light

Universal design sheds new light on the importance of good lighting. Lights in the right places and at the right level of brightness make a safer, more positive home environment, avoiding accidents and making residents feel cheerier and healthier.

Overall, or ambient, lighting is the first essential of the lighting plan. It needs to fill a room evenly and completely, from corner to corner, to reveal the full area and provide clear orientation. For balanced, shadow-free illumination, use central fixtures, perimeter cove lights, and wall fixtures with translucent covers that reflect light off a white or light-colored ceiling. It's fine to garnish this general lighting with decorative lamps or with accent lights, such as track lights, that are focused on artwork or other interesting room elements. Just don't count on these ornamental fixtures for ambient lighting.

The second essential is task lighting. Supplement the general lighting with targeted, task lights at reading corners, workstations, bathing areas, kitchen appliances, and wherever close vision is necessary. Direct this lighting across the task surface, perhaps from the sides, to prevent glare and over-the-shoulder shadows. Strips of small, undercounter task lights work well in the kitchen, especially when nonreflective, matte-finish countertop materials are used.

Mix It Up

Good lighting involves natural as well as artificial lighting. Daylight from windows and skylights makes spaces feel bigger, fresher, and more uplifting. For an even wash of natural light, distribute windows along more than one wall of the room—or at least place mirrors on walls facing windows. To moderate the intensity of sunlight, you can install awnings and deep eaves on the outside. On the inside, use window coverings, such as draperies and remote control window treatments. Glass blocks and frosted or textured glass are good options for windows and doors where light is welcome but privacy is important. Skylights set at an angle or covered with frosted glass provide more indirect, diffuse sunlight.

As we get older, we need more light to see sharply and perceive colors and objects accurately. Adequate natural light helps, as does artificial lighting that approximates daylight. Compact fluorescent bulbs, without the harshness and fluttering of earlier fluorescents, and LEDs (light emitting diodes) now can be used in place of standard incandescent bulbs, and come in a variety of temperatures (measured in degrees kelvin, or K), some of which can deliver "truer" colors and increase visual acuity. Another advantage of these new bulbs is that they last a long time; homeowners find themselves on stools changing bulbs less often. Randall Whitehead, of Randall Whitehead Lighting Inc., recommends 3,000 to 3,500K for general overhead lighting; 5,000K for windowless clothes closets; 2,700 or 3,000K for accent lights; and 2,700K for decorative fixtures. For good task lighting in the kitchen, go with 2,700 or 3,000K lights. Lighting at the bathroom mirror is best at 5,000K for daytime use and 2,700K in the evening. With dimmer switches, you can tailor the lighting as needed.

For a truly user-friendly lighting landscape, try to keep the level of lighting relatively consistent throughout the house, and make sure that light switches are accessible at every room entry. That way, adjusting your eyes to different light levels and negotiating in darkness will not be necessary.

▶ Glass blocks can be used on exterior walls or interior dividing walls to admit light while protecting privacy. The large window openings in this shower pull natural light from different directions for balanced illumination.

PRODUCTS FOR THE BATH

◄ A flexible rubber curb that flattens underfoot or wheel presents no barrier for users, but keeps water inside the shower.

▼ Sinuous grab bars can be installed vertically, horizontally, or at an angle to provide support whether people are tall or short, seated or standing. The 3-foot (91.4 cm) –long bars come in brass, chrome, and a combination of the two.

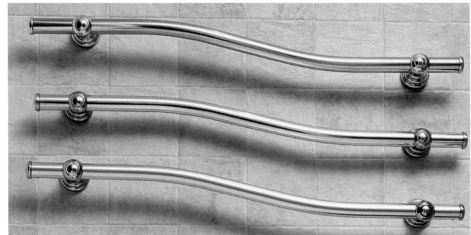

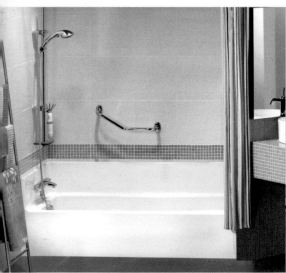

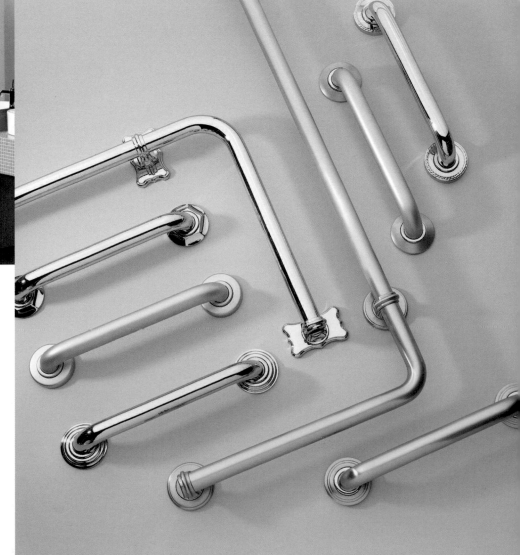

▲ Sized to fit into a standard tub niche, this tub/shower combo comes with a fold-down seat and grab bars already in place on the walls. The tub has air massage jets.

► Grab bars in assorted finishes, tones, configurations, and support styles coordinate with other bathroom accessories.

▼ Stylish and practical, the 24-inch (61 cm)-long polished chrome handhold on the tub deck matches the wavy 36-inch (91.4 cm)-long grab bar on the wall.

▶ When not in use, the shower seat folds against the wall. The rolling cart, available in single, stacked, and other modular configurations, brings towels and supplies wherever they're needed.

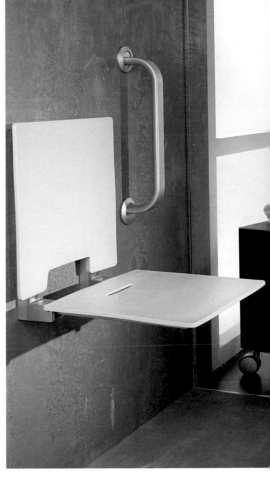

▲ Whichever direction you want to face, this shower bench is ready. Available with the longer seat on the right or left, the bench can be folded out of the way. It comes in many colors.

◀ Modular units designed for bathroom safety include a tub seat with or without backrest, a perimeter grab bar, and a soap caddy that can be placed anywhere on the grab bar that is most convenient. The company uses recyclable materials.

▼ Sliding on a chrome bar that doubles as a grab bar, this handheld shower spray locks in place with a lever handle. It features a durable metal hose that, at 59 inches (1.5 m), is long enough for comfortable use standing or seated.

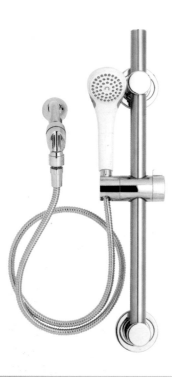

▼ A grab bar with an elbow provides support when transferring from a seated to a standing position. This one comes in an array of colors to coordinate with the bathroom design.

▲ Small enough to fit in a small bathroom, this pedestal sink integrates counter space on both sides and comes with accessible towel bars. The one-piece faucet—easy to use and appropriately compact—is a separate product.

◄ This classic-style bathtub faucet clusters the spout and handheld spray conveniently in one place on the tub deck. Available in several finishes, the unit comes with a 5-foot (1.5 m)-long metal hose for the spray.

▼ These easy-to-grasp lever handles feature an elegant profile that adds sparkle to the bathroom. One example of the wide range of attractive lever-style faucets available, the center-set unit comes in a satin or polished chrome finish that is treated to wipe clean easily.

▼ Console, or table-style, sinks naturally provide legroom for seated users. This slim, rounded unit brings the user close to the faucet, has sizable counter space, and has no sharp, protruding corners.

▲ A pivoting shower door opens outward for clear passage, and inward for access to the controls when preparing to shower. The shower enclosure incorporates controls reachable whether seated or standing; a built-in bench; accessible storage with rail to prevent things from falling out; a well-placed grab bar with slip-resistant finish; and jets opposite the controls—and behind the inwardly opened door—to avoid bursts of hot water when turning on the shower. Options include halogen lighting to illuminate the lower part of the enclosure.

◀ When the bathroom gets dark, the soft blue light in the bottom of the cabinet door goes on automatically; it can be operated manually as well. Tucked in the door fingerpull, the LED light is nonglare but bright enough to illuminate the area for safety.

▼ Low in cost, simple to apply, and smart to use, adhesive-backed safety treads in assorted designs make the tub and shower less slippery.

▼ Sitting and rising from this one-piece, water-saving toilet is eased by the elongated profile and contoured, chair-height seat. The toilet comes in many colors; the Power lite model comes with a heated seat for added comfort.

▶ Sophisticated design and a choice of stylish brushed nickel, oil-rubbed bronze, and polished chrome finishes make this grab bar a handsome addition to bathrooms or other areas of the house. The bar comes in a range of sizes and matches a line of faucets and bath accessories.

With a low threshold, slip-resistant floor, integrated seat and soap shelf, this molded, one-tone shower enclosure is crafted for safety and good looks. Available in many colors and subtle shades to complement other bathroom fixtures, the 48-inch (1.2 m)-wide, tile-look enclosure can be ordered with matching grab bars and handheld spray.

Grab bars that coordinate with company's faucets and accessories come with chrome and polished brass accent rings to broaden the design possibilities. Engineered with a special flange for secure attachment, the grab bars are available in lengths 12 to 36 inches (30.5 to 91.4 cm) long.

Enjoy luxury as well as safety and comfort in a shower package that combines your choice of elements, from custom-placed overhead, body, and handheld sprays to steam showerheads, waterproof speakers, and multicolor ambient lighting.

Well-suited for a seated user, this vessel, or countertop, sink has a shallow bowl and low-splash rim. The sink-mounted faucet features easy-grip lever handles and a high spout that won't be in the way. Wall-mounted faucets offer another option.

INDOOR/
OUTDOOR LIVING

Even from the outside, universal design homes extend a warm welcome. Thoughtfully designed entries invite people to come indoors, just as smooth transitions from the inside beckon them back outside to patios, decks, and yards.

A well-designed front entry is broad, bright, sheltered, and easy to approach—all without sacrificing good looks. A roof over the entry provides cover from rain and snow, while creating a sense of arrival. Attractive perimeter railings, bench seating, and a shelf for packages add character and convenience. Overhead lighting or sconces suffuse the entry area with an appealing glow that illuminates the doorway and helps identify the entry from the street. Small auxiliary lights trained on the address, doorknocker, and lock, and a lighted doorbell, also are helpful.

▶ The boundary between indoors and outdoors melts away here, to the benefit of both. Large bifold doors pull aside from the flush threshold to unite the indoor living area with the spacious covered deck. Floor-to-ceiling windows, glass doors, and interior transoms bring natural light and views inside. A balance of indoor and outdoor lighting helps meld the spaces, making both seem larger and creating a safer environment.

A large platform makes the entry feel substantial and function well. The smooth-paved platform should be roomy enough for several people to gather under cover at the door and include enough space on the open side of the door for someone using crutches, a walker, a wheelchair, or a stroller to maneuver. A wide entry door enhances the sense of place and user comfort. The door should be at least 3 feet (.9 m) across to facilitate entry by wheelchair users and others, and flanked by a sidelight or two to allow homeowners to see who's there. Peepholes, at heights suitable for all the home's occupants, provide extra security.

At least one entry, ideally including the front entry, should be free of steps. If the house is on a hill, let the car do the climbing by running the driveway up to the level of the house. In new construction, digging a deeper basement or dropping the foundation can reduce or eliminate the typical step into the main floor. A low-threshold replacement door smoothes the way.

Down to Earth

If the ground slopes up to the house, grading can ease the incline, allowing gently rising pathways to be used instead of steps. Another earth-moving strategy is to build a berm alongside the house as a platform for a wide, paved ramp. An inclined path with a shallow enough rise does not require handrails. Decorative shrubs can mark the edge of the path and buffer it from the street. Raised plant beds will do the job, too, and can provide a subtle handhold.

Railings, border walls, and even ramps can be built using materials or motifs that complement the house. A nicely crafted brick or redwood ramp, for instance, adds sophistication as well as safety to an entry. If steps are unavoidable, shallow risers, deep treads, and double handrails will make them user friendly.

The front walk and other paths outside the house should be at least 3 feet (.9 m) wide and paved with a smooth, hard material such as concrete, asphalt, or close-spaced bricks or flagstones in a cement bed. A smooth surface with a broom or textured finish will not present a slipping or tripping hazard. The wide paths will accommodate a parent and toddler walking side by side as well as an individual using a wheelchair or walker. A barely perceptible slope will be enough to aid rain runoff. Lighting along the walkway adds drama and improves visibility.

Smooth Transitions

Make the trip from car to house safe, simple, and stylish. Design a curb-free transition from driveway to walkway, with plenty of room for car passengers to disembark. If space is available, provide a roofed driveway section or carport and a covered walkway to shelter the way from the car to the door. Make the parking pad large enough that the driver can simply circle around to depart. Include maneuvering room for peo-

ple in the garage, too—at least 3 feet (.9 m), preferably more, around each car for passengers getting in and out. Allow more space for clear access to storage or hobby corners. Extra-high garage ceilings and doors can accommodate tall vehicles such as campers and vans with wheelchair lifts.

Patios, decks, and outdoor rooms enable everyone to enjoy the fresh air and views. Wide sliding doors or French doors with low thresholds provide an easy transition to outdoor living areas. For the most versatility, include areas that get full sun as well as more shaded places. A deep roof overhang may be enough to afford shade and protection from a summer shower. For decks, choose surfacing such as redwood, concrete, brick, or a wood-plastic composite that resists rot and mold. Leave only slim spaces between boards or bricks to permit drainage or expansion without catching heels, canes, or wheels. Ring the perimeter with narrowly spaced railings, benches, or planter

boxes. Give the patio or deck a slight slope for drainage.

For a seamless connection to the yard, bring the ground to meet the edge of the patio or low deck. If necessary, integrate a ramp into the deck to bridge the transition to ground level. Smooth pathways through the garden and around the property invite everyone to explore and enjoy the yard. Raised beds put the season's plantings in easy reach for most gardeners, eliminating the squatting and stretching. A ground cover of ivy, phlox, or even wood chips takes lawn maintenance out of the homeownership equation.

▼ Tiny lights show the way up the smooth bluestone path to this house and identify the edges of the walkway and steps; these lights happen to be removable, but permanent path lights can be installed. The user-friendly approach features a large ground-level platform; a wide stairway with shallow, 6-inch (15.2 cm) risers and generous, 12-inch (.3 m)-deep steps; a spacious, covered entryway; and a wide, well-lighted doorway.

The Roof That Isn't

Simply omitting the roofing in one corner adds a lot to this deck. The homeowners gain a place to sit in the sun, and the expanded view enhances the entire deck. The redwood beams, concrete floor, and metal railing are weather and insect resistant. Copper flashing gives the redwood extra protection from the elements.

NATURAL BEAUTY

Lush gardens greet visitors at the front of this house, and lush gardens surround them in the verdant backyard. The natural beauty here makes such a strong impression that the many outdoor accessibility features appear to be designed simply to enhance enjoyment of the gardens.

That's exactly the impression the homeowner hoped for when she landscaped the property. She wanted to be able to entertain guests in a refreshing, natural outdoor setting. And she wanted a landscape plan that gave her, as a wheelchair user, unrestricted access to the grounds without screaming that it was handicap accessible.

Architect Catherine Roha designed an easy-access entry approach that is both subtle and beautiful. There are two routes to the front door, one with steps and the other without. Visitors can walk up the steps and across a pathway to the covered entry. Stair rails emerge from columns that complement the Craftsman style of the house and are wired with recessed lights to illuminate the steps. The front walk intersects with the other route—a pathway that rises as a gentle ramp to the front door. The path criss-crosses the front yard like a Z so that it can achieve the 48-inch (1.2 m) rise from street level without becoming too steep.

Ramped Up

The first leg of the Z, a concrete ramp, blends with the sidewalk and inclines so mildly that no handrails are needed. Composed of redwood planks installed crosswise to avoid wheel-catching grooves, the other two legs have painted wood handrails that match those at the stairs. An offshoot of the ramp runs alongside the house to another no-threshold entry.

Flowering shrubs line the ramps, hiding them from street view and framing the assorted gardens that fill every patch of ground in front of the house. Traveling up the ramp is a botanical

adventure, including a raised planter box at the front door and such treats as a little garden of roses.

Something's always blooming in the backyard. Designed by the late Steven Alward, a landscape architect, and produced by Alward Construction, the backyard landscape features low-maintenance plants that bloom at various seasons, and a dynamic mix of garden beds, structures, and pathways. Oriented toward a far corner of the lot to broaden the circulation area and add visual interest, the plan encompasses a roomy redwood deck, a hot tub, a grassy area, a pergola, and an expanse of flagstone hardscaping interspersed with plant beds.

Alward incorporated level changes to enliven the design, with numerous ramped pathways that give the owner a choice of routes as she moves around the garden. To facilitate gardening, the plant beds are raised and are shaped to be accessible from more than one side. The homeowner can entertain on the large, sunny deck or enjoy shade and tranquility in the covered pergola.

Included on the homeowner's backyard wish list were three specific requests—an accessible hot tub, an outdoor breakfast area, and a place to picnic on the grass. Alward's design delivers all three. A kitchen door opens to the deck, where the homeowner can bring out her breakfast. The hot tub is conveniently located at the deck, yet hidden from the neighbors by shrubbery. A chair-height wall around the tub incorporates a transfer bench; a hydraulic seat is available to ease the homeowner into the water, leaving room for guests to enjoy the tub at the same time. The lawn is chair height, too, as is the retaining wall around it. A transfer bench in that wall invites the homeowner to stretch out and sunbathe in the grass or enjoy a picnic.

▶ Concrete-embedded flagstones make a smooth but natural-looking pathway that meanders around garden plots. The homeowner can sit by the raised plant beds to tend her flowers.

▼ Whether they use the front steps or traverse the ramp, homeowner and guests wind up together at the front door. The bottom of the gradual, Z-shaped ramp is concrete to meld with the sidewalk; the other two sections, screened behind shrubbery, are more patiolike redwood planks.

Ramps to entries

Handails for steeper ramps

No-threshold entries

Smooth paving

Protective edging on path borders

Raised planter boxes

Transfer surfaces for seated users

Low-maintenance plantings

Walkway lighting

Covered area for outdoor seating

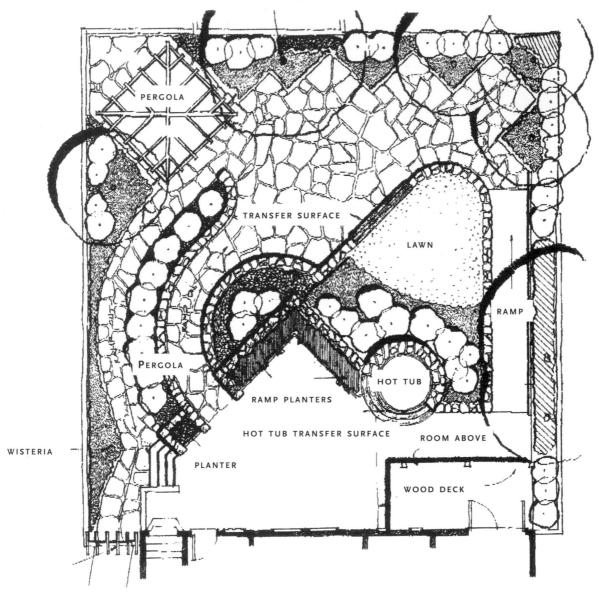

PERGOLA

TRANSFER SURFACE

LAWN

RAMP

PERGOLA

HOT TUB

RAMP PLANTERS

HOT TUB TRANSFER SURFACE

ROOM ABOVE

WISTERIA

PLANTER

WOOD DECK

NEW GATE WITH TRELLIS

▲ Several ramped pathways link the spacious deck to the gardens, lawn, and pergola. Retaining walls around the raised lawn and hot tub are at the chair height and a portion of each is topped with redwood for smooth transfer from a chair.

The Rugged Outdoorsy Look

The varied textures and irregular shapes of natural materials enrich the outdoor experience. Even though the paving and seating surfaces in this outdoor area are smooth and clean-cut, the landscape architect made a point of integrating natural, irregular features as well. He did it by applying rugged stones and rough-hewn redwood boards to vertical surfaces, such as the retaining walls of the raised plant beds and hot tub surround, where they add an outdoorsy texture without compromising safety.

TREE HOUSE

Children and adults alike get to sit in the trees at this house, and they don't have to shimmy up any trunks to do it. Melville Thomas Architects took advantage of the house's sloping site, extending the living area to a covered deck that perches among the treetops on story-high posts.

Where the ground slopes away behind the house, the deck begins. A wide entry leads directly from the kitchen to a screened and covered outdoor vestibule and onward to the screened deck. The living and dining rooms connect smoothly to the deck, too, via a 7-foot- (2.1 m)-wide outdoor corridor. Windows across the living space provide a visual link between indoors and out.

The shed roof of the main deck rises away from the house, embracing the sun and surrounding views. A flat roof over the connecting vestibule supplies continued shelter, while emphasizing the separateness of the tree house deck. Handsome, weather-resistant, painted steel railings with cypress handrails complement the cypress siding of the house and give protection without blocking views. Screens envelope both the deck and the vestibule. The Ipe deck surface is highly durable, well able to withstand weather extremes.

At 300 square feet (91.5 sq. m), the main deck is roomy enough for the whole family to gather for dinner; with the kitchen so close, bringing plates in and out is a snap. The deck has become one of the family's favorite places to relax together. And it's a natural draw for party guests, who come out to savor the wooded setting. Overhead fixtures light the exterior spaces and a ceiling fan keeps the breezes flowing. When conversation dies down, a stream can be heard rushing beneath the treetop getaway.

▶ Linked to the living space by an above-ground walkway, the roomy deck combines the shelter of a solid roof with the breeziness of open walls.

▲ The land slopes away, but the house keeps going on a level path out to the post-mounted screened porch.

▶ The soaring roof rises away from the house, opening the outdoor room to views all around and making it feel like a magical getaway, even though it is linked to the living space.

Access from more than one doorway

Wide, level pathway

Wide doorways

Lighted entry

3-foot (.9-m)-high railing

Covered deck for weather protection

Windows for visual connection to living spaces

Durable decking

GREAT OUTDOORS ROOM

The young family that lives here is as likely to invite guests outside as in. Nestled in the woods at the base of a mountain, the house celebrates its scenic surroundings. Architect Rick Jones, of Nash Jones Anderson Architects & Planners, designed an ingenious addition that allows family and friends to take in the view and enjoy the great outdoors, with all the comforts of home.

Attached to the house and open to it from the living room, the atmospheric timber frame addition is essentially an outdoor great room— that is, a family room/kitchen space without walls. A 30-by-18-foot (9.1 by 5.5 m) section of the L-shaped addition is set up as a seating area; another 21-by-20-foot (6.4 by 6.1 m) section is a kitchen complete with gas cooktop, barbecue, undercounter refrigerator, sink, bar, and dining table. Accessible, waterproof electrical outlets are distributed around the entire space, so the coffeemaker, blender, CD player, and television can be used outside.

Custom builder MWR Company crafted the robust, weather-resistant structure using Douglas fir posts and beams, masonry walls and a fireplace faced with local river rocks, a pine ceiling, and a smooth floor of bluestone embedded in concrete. Bluestone and river rock stairs lead down from the main house to the ground-level room, but a level concrete path from the driveway also is available.

Recessed ceiling lights illuminate the room in the evening, when the homeowners and their guests gather around the wood-burning fireplace. The raised hearth spreads the heat effectively and is easy to reach. Tucked under the stair landing, the wood box is conveniently nearby and accessible.

Short stone posts that match the walls and fireplace contain easy-to-tend raised planters. A garden adjacent to the driveway path can be planted with flowers or sheltering shrubs, to bring the beauty of the natural surroundings even closer.

▶ The timber frame ceiling structure offers shelter and a sense of enclosure. The focal point of the living room is the raised fireplace with integrated seating; glowing sconces on the posts enhance both the lighting and the living room ambiance.

▼ Attached to the main building, the open-air structure lets family and friends enjoy the outdoors without going far from the house. A level path with hardy cedar rail leads from the driveway to the outdoor room; a garden patch softens the visual impact of the path.

GREAT IDEA

Radiant Heat from Above

Radiant heaters hang from the ceiling to make this truly a four-season entertainment space. The climate here is moderate, but when temperatures get chilly, the homeowners flip a switch to make the outdoor room more comfortable. Since the heaters are radiant, they warm people and objects rather than taking on the impossible task of keeping the outdoor air toasty. Energy efficient to operate, the overhead heaters are out of reach of children and won't accidentally be brushed by passersby.

Level, concrete path from driveway

Smooth flooring

Durable, easy-care materials

Covered for rain and sun protection

Raised fireplace

Raised planters

Accessible appliances

Accessible, waterproof outlets

Overhead and task lighting

Radiant ceiling heaters

LEVEL BEST

Some locations are too good to give up, no matter how family circumstances change. When the owners of this property in the rolling countryside were newlyweds in the 1980s, the little house was just right for two. By the time the family had expanded to six, quarters were cramped. Rather than move, the owners hired architect Stewart Davis of CG&S Design-Build to design a children's wing and other additions, and remodel the house to assure easy living now and when the owners are older.

The new exterior of the house combines knockout styling with durability, easy mainte-nance, and smooth access. Davis used a bold combination of concrete block, limestone, and corrugated, galvanized steel—all tough and easy care—for the walls. The metal roofing and gutters also are long lasting and require little upkeep. All the new windows are energy-efficient, low-maintenance, aluminum-clad wood units, and the decks are paved with Ipe, an extremely hardy wood that resists rot, mold, and insects without treatment with toxic chemicals.

A large swath of smooth, stained concrete runs from the driveway to the front door. No driveway curb or entry threshold breaks the flow. A curved roof arches across the full width of the concrete platform, clearly identifying the entry and enabling several people to take shel-ter from the rain. The concrete pad has plenty of space for a bench and for wheelchair or walker maneuverability. Downlights on the out-side wall, lights that beam toward the curved ceiling, and interior lighting that shines through the windows and glass door combine to pro-vide well-distributed, glare-free lighting in the entryway. The wide driveway circles around an existing tree, saving the tree and making it easy to come and go without turning the car around.

Family members and guests can circulate from outside to inside and room to room without encountering any steps in this house. That's because CG&S graded the property to prepare a level surface radiating out from the existing structure to the additions, decks, garage, driveway, and guest parking area. All the exterior doors—3-foot (.9-m)-wide doors at the front and side, and patio doors in the back—are accessible, low-threshold models. A protective, covered gallery leads from the garage to the side entry and to the spacious backyard deck. With entries on three sides, expansive windows, and a suite of decks and galleries that open the remodeled house to the outdoors, the homeowners are prepared to enjoy this scenic property fully even when the children move on and it has become a home for two people again.

▼ A generous lighted archway across the front of the main house distinguishes the entry. The glass door and windows not only share the light but also allow the homeowners to see who is at the door. Exterior grading created a level surface from the driveway to the entry platform at the front door.

Level entry

Wide entry doors

Lever door handles

Covered entryway

Lighted entries

No curb between driveway and walkway

Covered breezeway

Low-threshold exterior doorways

Durable, low-maintenance paving

Level circular driveway

Accessible guest parking

▲ This wide covered gallery provides sheltered passage to the side door of the house. Highly durable Ipe hardwood flooring complements the stained pine ceiling; light fixtures illuminate the floor and provide broader lighting reflected off the angled ceiling.

GREAT IDEA

Covered Drain

Since steps or a raised threshold are not there to form a weather barrier at the entry, the remodeler ran a French drain, or linear gravel trench, across the front of the property to channel rainwater away. The drain slices through the concrete pad, but the 1 foot (.3-m)-wide gap doesn't interrupt the smooth entry. Why? It's covered with a metal grate that's flush with the concrete and has openings so narrow they won't catch heels or wheels.

PLAYING OUTSIDE

Turning this one-story, 1956 house into a family-friendly home involved turning the plan around and moving the focus from the formal living spaces in the front to the activity hubs: the informal kitchen, playroom, and backyard. Architect Ira Frazin shifted the kitchen to the rear of the house, stretching it between a new master bedroom wing on one side and a large new playroom/study wing on the other. The kitchen and both wings open to a spacious patio and pool deck.

Extra-wide, flat-threshold, sliding glass doors open the playroom to the patio, giving the family's three young children the free-flowing indoor/outdoor access they need in an area where the weather is usually warm. A large window and another set of wide patio doors punctuate the kitchen wall. With this visual connection and circulation link, the parents can work in the kitchen and still see, supervise, and interact with the children whether they are in the playroom or outside.

The patio is large enough to accommodate patio furniture and have room left over for the children to play. The kitchen doors make it convenient for the family to bring dinner fixings outside to cook on the built-in gas grill. Beyond the main patio square, the smooth concrete pavement wraps around the swimming pool and over to double doors at the master bedroom, inviting the homeowners to step outside for a morning dip.

Extended eaves shield all the entries, and a retractable awning offers extra protection from rain and sun. There's even a misting system to provide relief on hot, dry days. Floodlights illuminate the entire patio in the evenings, and wall fixtures brighten doorways. Interior lights shine through the surrounding windows and glass doors to suffuse the patio with a golden glow.

▼ Sliding doors meet at the corner, establishing an indoor/outdoor flow from the playroom to patio to kitchen. The retractable awning covers this activity hub. The master bedroom enjoys private access to the patio and pool.

GREAT IDEA

Removable Fence

While the children are young, placing a safety fence around the pool is essential. When they get older, it would be nice to remove the fence for a cleaner aesthetic. Both can be accomplished using PVC posts, with netting between, that fit into holes in the decking to make a safety fence around the pool. To remove the fence, the lightweight but sturdy posts can be pulled out; the decking holes are so small that they don't pose a safety issue.

Wide doorways

Low thresholds

Access from several parts of house

Low-maintenance, nonskid concrete paving

Gate around pool

Retractable awning

Protective roof overhangs

Lighting at doorways

Misting system for heat moderation

CHOICE ENTRIES

They wanted one-floor living but couldn't bear to leave their beloved nineteenth-century, two-story home. So instead of moving out, the owners of this house moved over, expanding their options with a fully equipped new first-floor wing. The core of daily living—entry, kitchen, and casual dining area—and a master suite have been shifted into the elbow-shaped addition. With the old building available, too, the house features a host of living arrangements for homeowners, guests, and helpers.

Design-builder Thomas Buckborough of Thomas Buckborough & Associates strategically arranged all the exterior access points for the addition. A roomy new garage sits at the elbow bend, equally convenient to the kitchen on the public side of the new wing and to the private master bedroom, bath, and office area. A roof extension covers the walkway that runs along the addition from the garage to the original house, providing shelter and visually completing the link between old and new. The walkway is wide enough for wheelchair, walker, or stroller. With room for bench seating along the wall, it can even be used as a little porch. Recessed cans illuminate the walkway; weather-safe, push-button switches operate the overhead lights, and are spotlighted themselves by a wall lamp at the entry door. A trellised roof continues the porch overhang to the garage doorway. Full sunlight brightens this spot now; vines will filter the light once they become established.

On the other side of the addition, double doors swing open for smooth, curbless access to the backyard patio.

A large, level driveway courses past the house to the garage. The driveway incorporates guest parking space and plenty of room for cars to turn around. Buckborough molded the ground from the driveway to the porch, forming a smooth, curbless transition at each end of a gently sloped pathway. He covered the path and the porch with smooth slate pavers securely embedded in concrete. The porch slopes slightly away from the house for drainage.

Windows in the garage doors, above them, and on a long garage wall bring natural light to this otherwise dim space. A wide doorway from the garage makes another curbless route between the driveway and house.

▼ The broad, level driveway connects seamlessly with the garage doorway and front walk. Because it rises gently, the walkway does not require handrails.

Entries on many
sides of house

Flat threshold
entries

Covered walkways

Wide, smooth paths

Graded pathways

Lighted doorways

Level driveway

Curbless driveway-
pathway connection

Maneuvering room
in driveway

Well-lighted garage

▲ A solid roof protects the entry porch; trellis-work over the garage access door adds natural light and visual relief.

Strategically Placed Exterior Door

One exterior doorway lends extra flexibility to the new wing. It opens from the office area of the master suite to the outdoors. If necessary, the office and its small adjacent bath could be turned into an apartment for a caregiver. The exit door would work as an apartment door.

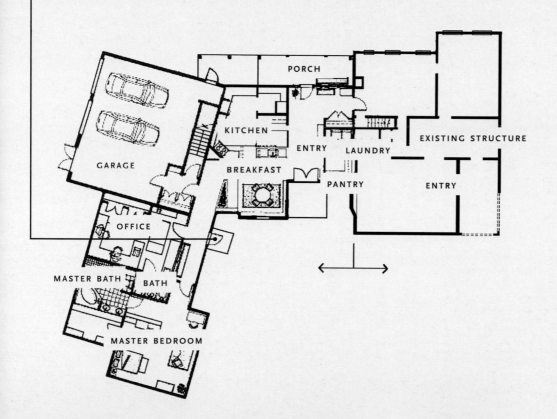

▲ Flush thresholds at the porch, garage, patio, and bedroom suite provide convenient, accessible entry points for homeowners, visitors, and helpers.

◄ A wide slate-paved porch links the garage to the entry. With a glass door, overhead lighting, and a lamp above the doorbell and light switches, the entry is easy to see and traverse.

Gallery

ENTRYWAYS

Entryways designed for a variety of users can be especially commanding and handsome. They are wide, well-lighted, and augmented with windows, roofs, rails, and other elements that make an architectural statement.

▶ Wide and welcoming, this covered entryway extends beyond the doorway to become a little porch, featuring benches that double as package platforms. No curb or high threshold obstructs the smooth flow from the driveway to a brick floor to an extra-wide, 3-foot 6-inch (1.1 m) door.

▼ Rather than break the clean linear roofline with a protruding entry, the remodeler of this rambler recessed the entry under the roof overhang. Additions on both sides angle away from the door to make room for a broad entry platform.

Glass Storefront Doors

Because this apartment has windows on only one side, the patio entry needed to do double duty—providing easy access and admitting as much natural light as possible. Low-maintenance aluminum and glass storefront doors with a flush threshold form a wall of light, and open a full 6 feet (1.8 m) wide to integrate indoor and outdoor areas for entertaining. A safety glass canopy over the doors offers weather protection without blocking the sun.

Gallery

PATIOS AND DECKS

Smooth transitions and versatility are the defining features of successful patios and decks. They provide an easy flow from indoors to outdoors, shade to sun, and patio to yard.

▶ Patio and yard come together here in an expansive wood platform that covers the irregularities of the ground, yet is close to ground level. The patio includes a covered section as well as extensions that bring gardeners closer to flowerbeds. Shallow ramps into the yard and house could also be added.

▼ When the 12-foot (3.7 m)-wide glass pocket door slides into the wall, this outdoor room merges with the living area within; a shallow threshold for water deterrence is the only divider. The tile-look flooring is low-maintenance formed concrete, stained and sealed. The barbecue counter and built-in round table also are easy-care concrete. Stamped steel louvers can be closed by flipping a switch to make a solid roof panel for weather protection. The perimeter structure overhead incorporates recessed fixtures and speakers for surround sound and light.

Gardener's Delight

This backyard system was designed with active as well as armchair gardeners in mind. A covered pathway from the garage and house connects to a sunny terrace and to a level, open-air path flanked by easy-access flower gardens. The path merges with the graded yard, where clay soil provides a firm surface. Galvanized planters and raised concrete beds bring garden patches into comfortable reach of the gardener, whether seated or standing. Admirers can enjoy the garden from the terrace, or from the porch, which was built onto the garage instead of the house to capture a great view without blocking light to the living spaces.

◀ Distinguished by corner posts, smooth stone pavers, and overhead trelliswork, this spacious outdoor room will enjoy both fresh air and shade when vines cover the arbor.

Gallery

PATHWAYS AND PAVING

The design and materials selected for patios and pathways take their cues from the architecture and setting. As long as the surface is smooth, hardy, and wide and level enough for easy navigation, the choices are plentiful.

▶ Gentle curves add interest and soften the effect of a concrete walkway without making it difficult to negotiate. The I-shaped brick pavers interlock to form a stable, rut-free surface. An edging of low, dense shrubbery contains the walkway yet retains the view.

Garage-to-House Connection

The garage is here, the house is there, and never the twain shall meet. Or shall they? In this case, a handsome covered ramp links the two. Constructed with cedar shingle siding, hardy Brazilian redwood flooring, and green-trimmed roof sections to complement the Arts and Crafts–style house, the 4-by-4-inch (10.2 × 10.2 cm)-wide pathway dresses up the entry and offers a scenic view of the yard as it shields people from the weather. Recessed fixtures light the passageway at night. The railing, crafted of red-painted metal rods and rustproof galvanized-steel panels in an Arts and Crafts motif, provides a decorative accent while guarding the ramp and deck.

◄ There's no need to iron the irregularities and character out of a yard to make it easily navigable. This raised wooden boardwalk "floats" above tree roots and uneven ground to establish a smooth, level pathway from the house to the patio.

3067

Welcome Ramps

Do you need a ramp to your door? Perhaps not: Grading or shaping the land, and dropping the foundation during construction, often can smooth away the steep approaches around a house so that ramps and steps are unnecessary. If you do plan to build a ramp, design it for looks as well as safety. Choose a design motif that coordinates with the house, and apply the following structural recommendations. Check your local code for setback requirements and any variations from these guidelines.

The gentler the rise, the easier a ramp is to use. Most guidelines say the slope should be no steeper than 1:12, or 1 inch (2.5 cm) of incline for every 12 inches (30.5 cm) of ramp length. Shallower ramps, such as 1:16, are even easier to negotiate, and ramps with a steady slope of just 1:20 are so gentle that they don't usually require handrails or protective borders. Consistency is important; that is, ramps should rise at a steady angle. Shallower ramps, such as those 1:17 to 1:20, should incorporate a level landing for rest every 40 inches (101.6 cm). Steeper ramps, in the 1:12 to 1:16 range, need a landing every 30 inches (76.2 cm) along the way.

◄ With crisp white handrails that match the porch rail, this shallow ramp harmonizes with the style of the house and adds character to the entry. The ramp bridges a gully that's shielded with flowering shrubs, but plantings would dress up the base of any ramp. The house was built by Atlanta Habitat for Humanity, which has provided accessible entrances to all of its new houses since 1989.

Ideally, the ramp should be a straight run from the bottom to a covered landing at the top, where there is at least a 5-foot (1.5 m) turning radius to give wheelchair users room to turn around and open the door. In order to rise gradually enough, though, some straight ramps would be too long for the yard. Depending on yard space and the length needed, these ramps can be set up as compact switchbacks, L-shaped structures, or longer, U-shaped pathways, again with a 5-foot (1.5 m) diameter level landing at each turning point.

To allow space for two people to walk side by side or a wheelchair user to hold the handrails, the clear floor surface of the ramp should be 4 feet (1.2 m) wide. The minimum recommended width is 3 feet (.9 m). For drainage, the surface can be sloped very slightly from the center to the sides or crosswise—up to 1:50. Protective curbs at least 2 inches (5.1 cm) high should border the ramp on both sides unless, of course, the wall of the house serves as a safety edge on one side.

Place guardrails on both sides, too. They should start below the ramp surface and reach 36 to 48 inches (.9 to 1.2 m) above the floor, with attached handholds 30 to 36 inches (76.2 to 91.4 cm) high. The handrails should be rounded for a comfortable grip, and be mounted 1 1/2 inches (3.8 cm) from the guardrail or wall. Extend the railings at least 12 inches (30.5 cm) beyond the ramp at each end, for maneuverability and spatial orientation. A horizontal strip near the bottom of the guardrail keeps feet or wheels from falling through, while allowing space for drainage, snow, and leaf removal. The upright posts of the rail on high ramps—those at least 18 inches (45.7 cm) above ground—need to be spaced fewer than 5 inches (12.7 cm) apart; there's more latitude on spacing if the ramps are closer to the ground.

What material should you use for the ramp? Choose a surface that is durable, nonskid, and appropriate for the style of the house. Nonslip brushed or broom-finish concrete offers a sturdy look. Smoothly laid interlocking bricks are more traditional. Synthetic wood-look products are long lasting. Pressure-treated wood can be stained and weatherproofed or painted with slip-resistant, grit-impregnated paint. Accent the ramp with painted railings, shrubs, and flower boxes that raise the ramp to star status as a landscape element.

HOME TOURS: WHOLE-HOUSE DESIGNS

To get a real sense of the livability and appeal of homes that incorporate universal design features, it's helpful to step in and poke around. This chapter takes you on a tour of many wonderful, widely diverse residences, all designed for comfort, ease of use, and joy of surroundings.

You will explore compact apartments as well as houses small and large; one-floor and multistory homes; remodeled and new houses in assorted styles on a variety of sites; custom designs and a home builder's demonstration model; luxurious and more budget-conscious designs.

As a group, they share certain universal design musts—open circulation areas, good lighting, and easy-to-reach appliances, fixtures, and storage. They also include sensible features such as smooth flooring, low thresholds, lever-style and other easily gripped door and cabinet handles, and conveniently located outlets and rocker light switches.

Yet each has special features and a spark of originality that give it character, uniqueness, and personality.

Even more motivating and thought provoking is the wide range of residents in these homes. One was designed for a family with young children. Others are homes for baby boomers and older adults living busy, independent lives. Some owners designed their homes to accommodate particular mobility issues. Still others invested in "future-proofing" to ensure that both they and their guests will always be able to function in their homes with ease.

As these homes show, universal design works in every setting, for any resident, to make homes versatile, adaptable, and accessible. Their beauty demonstrates that universal design in no way diminishes creative possibilities.

▶ In the master bath of this house, the shower is a seamless, curbless extension of the room with an integral bench and a glass block privacy panel.

▶ Glazed pocket doors provide a wide, no-threshold entrance to the office and let natural light from office windows shine through to the living area.

▲ A wash of terra-cotta–colored paint on built-in cabinets and walls lends visual cues as well as stylistic punch in the open living space of this house, designed by CG&S Design-Build.

MASTER PLANNING

After decades of researching, teaching, and writing about what he calls transgenerational design, Jim Pirkl designed and built a user-friendly house for his own family. Needless to say, it is masterful. A good transgenerational house makes living easy for young and old, able and disabled. A great one anticipates the needs of all without sacrificing architectural beauty. Pirkl's contemporary 2,700-square-foot (250.8 sq. m) house is both handsome and chock-full of cutting-edge features that enhance convenience and accessibility.

A retired design professor who now owns a company called Transgenerational Design Matters, Pirkl built a house in which he and his wife would be comfortable living on their own, and that their children and future grandchildren would enjoy visiting. Perched on a high plateau, the one-story, C-shaped house soaks in exhilarating mountain views and embraces a sheltered, yet sun-filled, courtyard. A covered patio wraps around the courtyard to provide shady seating areas and shield windows from solar heat gain. At one end of the C, the master suite opens to the courtyard. At the other end, the living area/entertainment space extends to the courtyard. Overnight guests, who stay in the center of the C, can step out to the courtyard without migrating into the owners' private wing. The courtyard area includes a slim, shallow pool that the Pirkls use for daily exercise but that guests, including children, enjoy as well.

Easy Landing

Though the property is high on a hill, the buildings and landscaped grounds are basically on the flat. Pirkl sees the driveway as essentially an elevator, carrying everyone up to the broad parking pad, garage, and house. The garage floor slopes 4 inches (10.2 cm) to facilitate drainage, and allows no-step access to the house. Pirkl built a jumbo three-car garage, reserving one bay for a hobby workshop furnished with an adjustable closet organizer system and wheelchair-accessible workbench space.

A smooth, paved walkway, again slightly sloped for drainage, leads to the wide, well-lighted, and weather-protected front entry alcove. The open living and dining areas are conveniently located near the entry. Between the two spaces, Pirkl suspended from the ceiling an oversize antique post office box panel that serves as both conversation piece and room divider. Since it does not touch the floor, the divider defines the spaces without obstructing floor area or blocking light. Likewise, wall-mounted cabinets in the dining area provide the benefits of a buffet and china cabinet without limiting circulation. The sideboard supplies a supporting surface for people with mobility concerns, and the space underneath works as a deep toe kick, enabling wheelchair users to get close to the buffet.

Circulation space is generous and unencumbered throughout the house. A system of sunlit hallways, 42 to 60 inches wide (1.1 to 1.5 m) wide, links all areas, providing clear passage by wheelchair users and others. All interior doors are 36-inch (.9 m)-wide , no-threshold units, many of them space-saving sliders on easy-glide hardware. All rooms, even small ones, incorporate 5-foot (1.5 m)-diameter turnaround areas so that wheelchair users can go anywhere in the house and not have to back out.

Kitchen on the Move

In the kitchen, a deceptively simple line of cabinets and appliances, raised 10 inches (25.4 cm) off the floor, forms a ring around a wide-open central core. The room is a dynamic mix of movable components. A cutting board surface tucked into one corner tops a docked trolley that can be moved around for use as an island, a counter extension, or a cart to transport heavy items. Above the trolley dock are wide dish drawers with flip-down front panels so that dishes can be slid out without lifting. Low pantry shelves for infrequently used items line the back of the trolley garage. Most of the other pantry items are contained in five tall pullout units, each open on the sides and furnished with adjustable racks so the contents are easy to see and accessible from both sides. For kitchen supplies, Pirkl designed full-extension drawers with 4-inch (10.2 cm)-high sides for easy viewing, and cutout handles for easy gripping. Cabinets around the room have graspable D-shaped hardware.

Instead of a vent hood, on which tall people like Pirkl can bump their heads, he opted for a cooktop with a popup vent. The microwave and convection ovens are stacked for convenient access and transfer of dishes; the oven has a counterbalanced door that can be opened without effort. When the oven timer rings, a light flashes in case the tone is not heard. And when the oven is not in use, a panel hides its controls from curious youngsters.

Removable cabinet doors below the 33-inch (83.8 cm)-high kitchen sink harmonize with the suite of doors and drawers around the room, and also enclose legroom area for seated users. With its top at 42 inches (1.1 m) above the floor, the dishwasher is comfortable for seated or standing users. Counters at three different heights—33, 36, and 42 inches (83.8 cm, .9 m, and 1.1 m)—provide options for a mix of uses and users. Pirkl designed a rounded lip for the edges of the lower counters to form a fingertip grab bar that can be used to steady oneself or

▲ Furnishings, rather than walls, define zones in the bright and open living/dining area. Cabinets suspended from the ceiling and mounted on the wall leave floor spaces clear and easy to clean.

pull out of a chair. He chose resilient cork flooring for the kitchen; nonglare, slip-resistant tile for the hallways; and bamboo for the other floors throughout the house, because it is beautiful and easy on the feet, yet hard enough to accommodate wheelchairs.

A mix of general lighting, task lighting, and natural light from windows and a skylight leaves no part of the kitchen in shadows.

For now, the Pirkls enjoy the convenience of having their washer and dryer at one end of the kitchen. The front-loaded machines are raised 10 inches (25.4 cm) off the floor and hide behind doors that match the rest of the kitchen cabinetry. Pirkl's wife, Sarah, likes to sit while ironing, and a table-height ironing board that pulls out and unfolds from a nearby drawer enables her to do that. There's pullout tray storage below. If the Pirkls decide to move the laundry out of the kitchen, the utility room by the garage is plumbed and ready.

Luxurious Bath

The master bath is nothing short of indulgent. A tub for soaking fills an entire wall. The tub's wide, chair-height surround provides seating or transfer space at both ends. The controls are front and center, where they can easily be reached from inside or outside the bath. At the back wall of the tub is a convenient pullout spray. Grab bars spaced symmetrically around the tub are attractive as well as functional.

An easy-open pocket door and pullout shelves separate the bathroom into two areas, one for the tub and vanities, and the other for a skylighted room that contains a commode and a roll-in shower. The shower is equipped with grab bars, a flip-down seat, and an adjustable-height showerhead. The shower's glass door

can be removed to turn the entire compartment into a luxurious wet room or make the shower even easier to enter. Here, and in the guest bath, the commodes are wall-mounted units with in-wall tanks; it's easier to clean the floor under off-the-floor toilets, says Pirkl. He installed them at chair height for accessibility and comfort, and flanked them with attractive grab bars. Blocking is in place behind the walls for grab bars to be installed later, if wanted.

Pirkl seized every opportunity to enhance convenience and independence in this house. The front door lock, the living room fireplace, and even the high window coverings operate by remote control. Door handles are levers, windows are crank-open casements, and light switches—lowered to 42 inches (1.1 m)—are rocker-style. Outlets, raised to 18 inches (45.7 cm), are plentiful and easily reached. The thermostats have easy-grip controls with large, easy-to-see numbers. The exercise pool is self-cleaning. Clearly, this is a home designed to be enjoyed by everyone.

◄ The crown jewel of the master bath is a soaking tub with accessible central controls and a wall-to-wall surround that offers seating or transfer space at both ends. Color-coordinated grab bars provide a convenient safety handhold for getting in and out.

Front-loading washer and dryer

Grab bars

Adjustable shelving

No-threshold doors

Curbless shower

Off-the-floor toilets

Foldaway ironing board

Remote-control gas fireplace

Remote-control window coverings

Lever door hardware

Accessible electrical switches

Adjustable-height sink system

Casement windows

Side-by-side refrigerator/ freezer

Automated skylights

Radiant floor heating

Cooktop with pop-up vent

Large digital thermostat

Sliding doors with easy-glide hardware

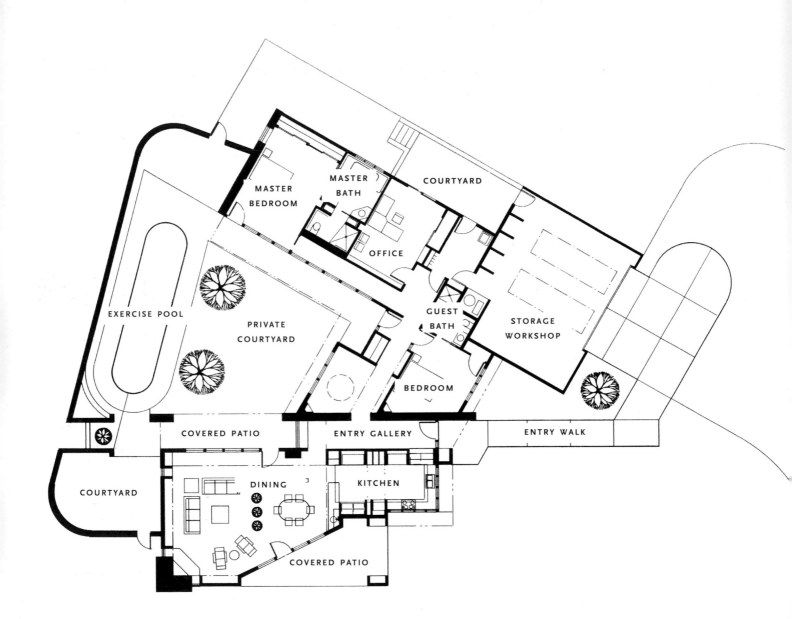

MASTER
BEDROOM

MASTER
BATH

COURTYARD

OFFICE

EXERCISE POOL

PRIVATE
COURTYARD

GUEST
BATH

STORAGE
WORKSHOP

BEDROOM

COURTYARD

COVERED PATIO

ENTRY GALLERY

ENTRY WALK

DINING

KITCHEN

COVERED PATIO

▲ The C-shaped 2,700-square-foot (250.8 sq. m) house separates the living area from private spaces while giving access from both to the central courtyard. Sliding glass doors provide additional light and access to patios and courtyards around the perimeter of the house.

GREAT IDEA

Pass-Through Shelf

There's no need to lug packages into this house. Outside the front door, Pirkl built a sheltered, chair-height wall recess to use as a package drop. One step inside the house and the Pirkls can transfer their packages onto a 42-inch (1.1 m)-high entryway shelf that serves as a pass-though to the kitchen. Arms free, they can go around the corner and slide the packages onto a kitchen counter. In the entry, a built-in seat under the pass-through can be used as a package drop or a place to sit down and remove boots.

Expanded View of Kitchen

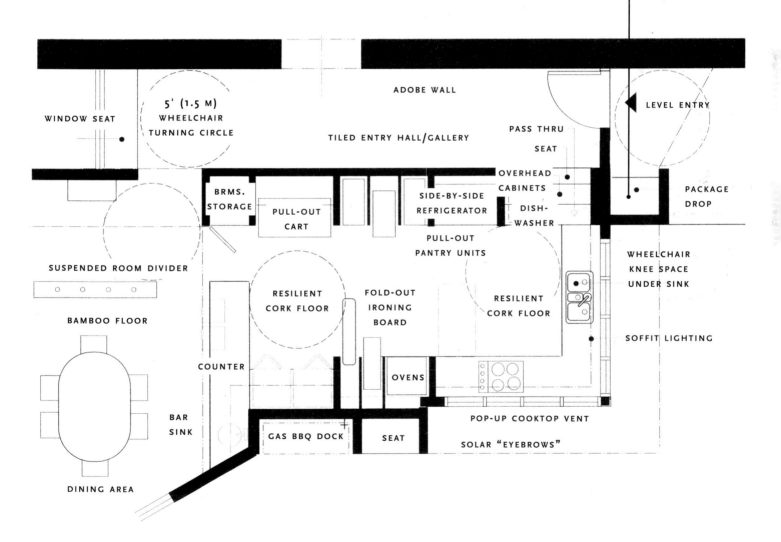

▲ Pirkl created a practical kitchen with a wide-open floor area and clean lines by using pullout storage units, a tuck-away cart, and door and drawer fronts to hide the washer, dryer, and ironing board.

GREAT IDEA

Adjustable-Height Vanities

A tall man, Pirkl installed his master bathroom vanity at 40 inches (102 cm) from the floor to minimize bending. His wife is shorter, so 33 inches (83.8 cm) is the comfortable height for her vanity. What if their needs or preferences change? Though topped with heavyweight Corian, both master bath vanities—and even the vanity in the guest bath—are adjustable. The wall-mounted vanities lock securely in place, but can be raised or lowered on a commercially available Pressalit track.

▲ The level, accessible courtyard offers a choice
of open-air and covered seating. Wide,
smooth, paved paths encircle the exercise pool
and the landscaped area, where raised plant
beds can be tended without back strain.

A NEW HOME STANDARD

Most home builders offer a choice of standard models to satisfy a variety of buyers. Centex Homes set a new standard with this house, tweaking one of its popular designs to create a single home in which many types of buyers—from families with young children to empty nesters, older adults, and persons with disabilities—will feel right at home.

The 3,500-square-foot (325.2 sq. m), two-story house is almost a dead ringer for its sister model; many of the modifications are essentially invisible. The bright, spacious rooms and inexpensive adjustments—wider doorways, raised appliances, lever-style handles, and easy-to-reach thermostat, electric panel, and light switches—give the house broad appeal, says architect Bill Devereaux of Devereaux & Associates. The design is not fully accessible, but nearly so, incorporating many universal design features.

From the outside, you'd never know the house was designed with accessibility in mind. Steps lead to the well-lighted covered porch and front door just like the other models on the street. There's a shelf by the front door to put down packages, but that's a convenience any buyer would like.

What you might not notice is that the house sits low to the ground, within 8 inches (20.3 cm) of grade, because Devereaux set the foundation more than a foot closer to the ground than is typically specified. One of the few major changes to the model, the lower foundation requires fewer front steps to the house, and behind a row of bushes is an alternate entry—a sloped walkway from the driveway with such a shallow incline that handrails aren't needed. Behind the house, Centex built up—or bermed—the ground to make a smooth, no-step transition from patio to yard. In the garage, a gentle, 5-foot (1.5 m)-wide incline with turning space

provides problem-free access from car to house. Another shelf, this one in the laundry/utility room, gives homeowners a place to perch packages when they enter from the garage.

Gracious View

A two-story entry foyer announces that this house has panache. Views extend from the entry through family room windows at the back of the house. The formal living and dining rooms open to one side, and private quarters for the homeowners occupy the other side of the main floor. Everybody loves the raised

hearth in the family room, which looks great and makes tending the fire easier. Built-in shelves in the living room look handsome, too, and are within reach for all.

Devereaux retained the open family room–kitchen plan, but made the circulation space broader in places for easy passage. Smooth hardwood covers all areas of the main floor, except the family room, which has low-pile carpet, and the bathrooms and laundry, which have easy-to-clean tile. All three flooring materials—and most of the other finishes and products in the house—are standard selections in Centex homes. The architect reshaped and widened the staircase to 48 inches (1.2 m), installing handrails on both sides so that two people can ascend side by side. Shallow risers and deep treads with a perimeter of dark wood around blond wood make the stairs user-friendly for children, the visually impaired, and those with mobility issues. Even with a landing, the stairs can accommodate a mechanical lift if needed.

Creative Spaces

The house has a roomy pantry at the juncture of the kitchen and entry hall. Directly overhead is a second-floor computer workstation. Stacking these spaces was no accident; they are sized so that a standard-size residential elevator can replace them if the homeowners choose. A pit for elevator mechanicals hides under a removable floor panel in the basement, ready to go.

Devereaux borrowed space from an adjacent study to expand the powder room, giving it a

◀ The house blends in with its neighbors, but is easier to enter because the foundation is set lower to the ground. From the front walk, the front porch is just two steps up. A smooth, wide, gently rising path leads from the driveway to the porch.

5-foot (1.5 m) diameter wheelchair turning circle and a luxurious ambiance. With an accessible powder room, guests need not penetrate the master suite in search of a large bathroom. Devereaux reconfigured and enlarged one of the upstairs bathrooms for accessibility and versatility, adding a built-in bench that works as a place to stack clothes for the day, or to sit for entry into the bathtub.

For the master bath, instead of the large corner tub and smaller shower in the look-alike model, Devereaux chose a large, roll-in corner shower and a standard-size tub. The shower controls are mounted by the shower entry, and are easy to reach from outside or in. An elegant beige tile surround contrasts with the white tub, making both easier to distinguish visually. Cutout cubbies in the tub-side bench keep towels handy. Each of the separate his-and-hers vanities has a large countertop, legroom beneath, and ample drawers to the side. Multiple outlets are arranged at the vanities, and a phone jack was placed by the commode. Blocking is in place behind the walls in this and the other accessible bathrooms so grab bars can be installed easily if needed.

Between the master bathroom and bedroom, a pocket door keeps the circulation space clear. Two walk-in closets flank the short hall between rooms. One of the closets has a pocket door as well; generously sized for wheelchair clearance, the closet contains a suite of adjustable shelves that any homeowner would relish.

Kitchen Transformation

A few strategic changes transform the kitchen into an activity center, where the family can gather and where more than one person can work. Two ovens, including a microwave/convection combo unit, are stacked at midwall for easy access. The adjacent cooktop, with legroom beneath, is set in a counter that has ample space for shifting pots from burner to oven or vice versa.

Devereaux enlarged the kitchen island to make it multifunctional. One section contains a table-height eating counter and a food-prep center with a sink that has undercounter legroom. Next to it are two stacked refrigerator drawers, inserted at an accessible height in a bar-height section of the island.

Countertops and cabinetry are in contrasting shades to be distinguished clearly by all. Undercounter cabinets contain full-extension drawers, and overhead cabinets have pull-down units to bring shelves into reach. There are two dishwasher drawers at the cleanup center, both reachable from a seated position. Unless company is coming, the homeowners may need to use only the top drawer, for even less bending and lifting. A pass-through to the family room lets homeowners join in conversation, and facilitates the job of transporting dishes to the sink.

▶ The wide stairway not only lends an air of graciousness to the house, it also is easier to negotiate because of the shallow risers, deep, two-tone treads, and double handrails.

No-step entries

Wide front door and hinged sidelight

Varied counter heights

Dishwasher drawers

Refrigerator drawers

Side-by-side refrigerator/ freezer

Roll-out kitchen and bath shelves

Pull-down shelves

Low cooktop with legroom for seated user

Pot filler behind cooktop

Front loaded washer and dryer

Roll-in shower

Accessible bathroom storage

Elevator-ready

Pocket doors

Lever handles

Accessible outlets and light switches

Adjustable closet shelves

Easy-to-use stairs

Upgrade: side-hinge oven door

GREAT IDEA

Hinged Sidelight

Even with a 30-inch (76.2 cm)-wide entry door, getting through the doorway can be a tight squeeze if you are loaded down with packages, or you're assisting someone else, or your refrigerator is being delivered. That's never a problem at this house because the sidelight by the front door is hinged. A standard 2-foot (.6 m)-wide sidelight, special ordered with a hinge, locks into place and swings open when a wider doorway is needed.

First Floor, Before

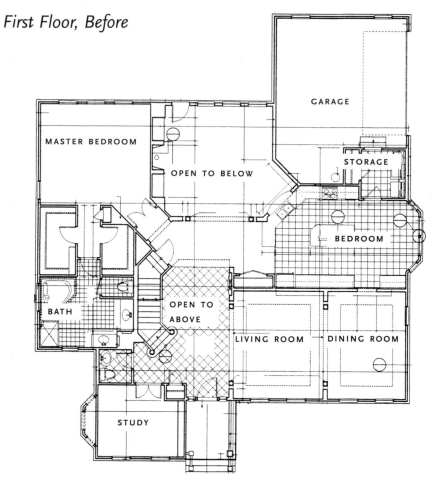

First Floor, After

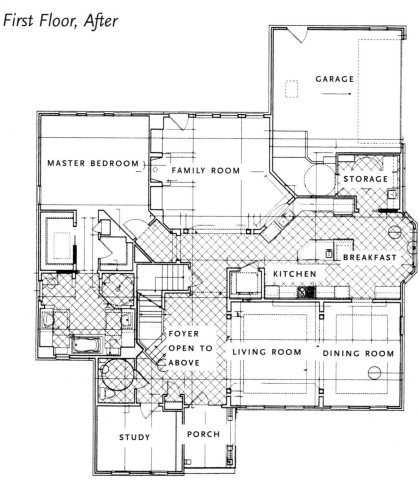

▲ Subtle changes, such as a larger powder room, wider doorways, and wider stairs converted this standard new home into a universal design model. The plan already had a main-floor master suite; in the new design, the rearranged and slightly larger master bathroom incorporates a roll-in corner shower and roomy, easy-access, his-and-hers vanities. One of the walk-in closets has a wider doorway and adjustable shelves.

Second Floor, Before

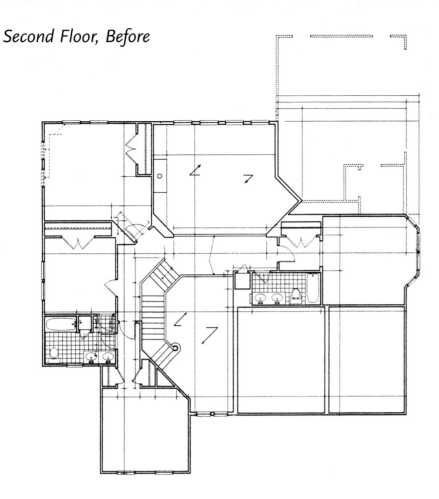

Second Floor, After

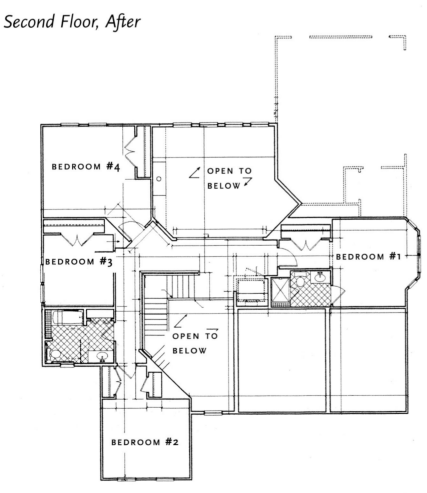

BEDROOM #4

OPEN TO BELOW

BEDROOM #3

BEDROOM #1

OPEN TO BELOW

BEDROOM #2

▲ Devereaux did not have to change the second floor plan much to introduce accessibility. He widened doorways, enlarged one bathroom, and shifted another bathroom to reserve room for an elevator shaft. For now, the elevator space is in use as a computer station.

▼ Devereaux enlarged the kitchen island to incorporate a roomy, table-height counter, plus a food-prep center with a sit-down space and adjacent refrigerator drawers. The cooktop also can be used from a seated position; food from adjacent ovens can be moved with ease to the counter.

SMALL APARTMENT, BIG APPEAL

Like most apartment buildings, this one is home to a wide assortment of people—young and old, some with physical limitations, most without. Yet the airy design and easy-living features of the apartments have drawn rave reviews from all the tenants alike.

It's a mission accomplished for developer McCormack Baron Salazar and Trivers Associates architect Greg Zipfel, who wanted to offer attractive, reasonably priced apartments with wide appeal and universal livability. The eighty units are not large—640-square-foot (59.5 sq. m) one-bedrooms and 1,100-square-foot (102.2 sq. m) two-bedrooms—but they use the space well. In each unit, the kitchen and living area share an open space brightened by floor-to-ceiling windows. Zipfel also used shared space between the bathroom and laundry to add elbowroom. In fact, he incorporated 5-foot (1.5 m)-diameter clearances throughout, so the apartments feel roomy and are wheelchair ready.

Ingenious accent walls in the two-bedroom units—featuring colorful panels framed by transoms and sidelights—enclose the bedrooms for privacy while allowing light to stream through. To preserve the flow of space and light in the one-bedroom units, where privacy is less necessary, a slimmer accent wall defines the sleeping area. All the doors in the apartments are 3 feet wide (.9 m) wide for accessibility, including the space-saving sliding doors between bedroom and bath.

Because the building is located in an area where warehouses are shoulder to shoulder with commercial and residential buildings, it made sense to design warehouse-style, high-ceilinged apartments. The tall ceilings have the advantage of enhancing the sense of openness and creating a broad area for large, warehouse-like windows that admit lots of natural light. Serendipitously, the super-size windows proved economical to construct because only one window opening—enclosing a window for the living area and another for the bedroom—needed to be framed. Each window area contains some operable, awning windows with lever handles.

On the Surface: Convenience

Using mostly off-the-shelf products, Zipfel designed an affordable kitchen that is a study in versatility and convenience. It's located by the apartment entrance so the kitchen counter is a nearby platform for packages and grocery bags. The dishwasher is installed 12 inches (.3 m) above the floor where the racks can be used from a standing position without bending. The oven is 18 inches (.5 m) off the floor, making the top rack the same height as the 3-foot (.9 m) counter so that casseroles can be shifted from oven to counter without lifting. Zipfel chose a smooth, glass cooktop to make it easy for users to slide pots on and off the cooking surface. The unit is $^1/_2$ inch (1.3 cm) higher than the countertop in which it is set, but pots can be shifted onto a trivet without being lifted. In place of the usual range hood switches mounted high on the hood itself, the wiring for the hood light and fan have been connected to an easy-to-reach rocker-style wall switch. There are plenty of electrical switches and outlets around the kitchen and the apartment, all within reach of a seated user.

Base cabinets contain pullout shelves to make full use of the available storage space and bring all items within reach. Corner cabinets house lazy Susans. Here, and in the bathroom, Zipfel incorporated toe kick space under the base cabinets that is a full 9 inches high (22.9 cm) and 6 inches (15.2 cm) deep. Not only does this make the cabinets accessible for wheelchair users; it also essentially enlarges the rooms by incorporating under-cabinet space as part of the 5-foot (1.5 m)-diameter open area recommended for wheelchair maneuverability.

Dark laminate countertops contrast with blond wood cabinets for good looks and easy-to-distinguish surfaces. Likewise, dark-painted baseboards elsewhere in the apartment add style and clearly mark room perimeters. The handsome floor—maple veneer on an engineered wood backing—is smooth, easy to maintain, and economical to purchase.

Good-looking, nonskid tile paves the bathroom/laundry floor. In the laundry area, front-loading appliances with front-panel controls are convenient for all, including seated users. In the bathroom, the shower base is recessed $^3/_4$ inch (1.9 cm) to achieve a low threshold for roll-in access. A few grab bars are sprinkled around the room, and blocking for others hides behind the walls Undercounter drawers are pressed to the sides of the vanity to allow seated users to approach the sink. A panel above the low towel bar flips down to reveal a handy compartment for toothbrush and toothpaste. Zipfel came up with a great way to place the bathroom sink with an off-center faucet within reach of children or seated adults: He specified a round bowl and simply rotated it 30 degrees off center.

▼ The living space is bright, open, and free flowing, with smooth wood-veneer flooring, wide doorways, and broad illumination from floor-to-ceiling windows. A privacy wall encloses the bedroom, but interior transoms and a sidelight pass light through.

Adjustable counter with hydraulic lift

Awning windows

Engineered wood flooring

Nonskid tile bathroom/ laundry floor

Accessible oven and cooktop

Raised dishwasher

Side-by-side refrigerator with water and ice dispenser

Pullout cabinet shelves

Lazy Susan corner storage

Grab bars

Roll-in shower

Bath vanity with legroom for seated user

Handheld shower spray

Round sink in bathroom

Front-loaded washer and dryer

Easy-grip handles

Ample toe kick space under base cabinets

Adjustable Kitchen Countertop

Ideally, a universal design kitchen has countertops of varying heights to suit different people and different functions. The compact kitchens in these apartments had no room for such an array of workstations. Instead, Zipfel teamed up with the contractor and developer to devise an adjustable counter on the end of the kitchen island. It can be raised or lowered with ease to any height, becoming a 27-inch (68.6 cm)-high sit-down table, a 44-inch (111.8 cm)-high bar top, and anything in between. The central post, bolted to the floor, is a pressurized hydraulic table base readymade for restaurants. Release a lever under the counter and the top rises; press gently on the top and it lowers.

▶ The vanity is ready for a seated user, with drawers on the right, a shallow medicine cabinet and undercounter toothbrush compartment on the left, a low towel bar, and an offset, easy-to-reach faucet.

◀ The tidily arranged kitchen is practical and user friendly. Appliances are mounted 1 foot (30.5 cm) off the floor for convenient access; cabinets are equipped with pullout shelves; electrical switches and outlets are plentiful and easy to reach; and the adjustable countertop lends the island limitless versatility.

Two-Bedroom Unit

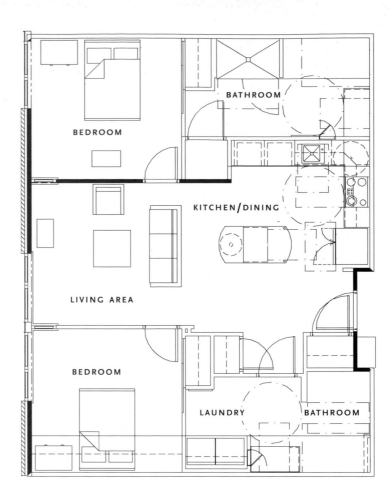

One-Bedroom Unit

▶ Open-plan living spaces and a shared floor area between the bathroom and laundry facilitate circulation and make these apartments live large. Each area of the apartments has a 5-foot (1.5 m) turning radius for wheelchair users.

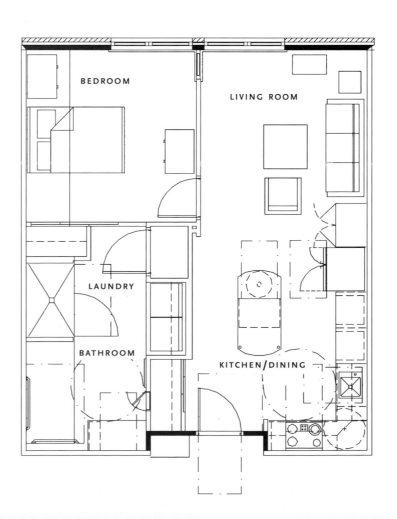

▲ The dishwasher racks are easy to reach from a standing or seated position. One of the oven racks is counter height, so carrying items from oven to island counter is as simple as turning around. The side-by-side refrigerator/freezer makes food items accessible.

LUXURY LIVING

After years of living in a grand, multistory Victorian, moving to a ranch house felt like a step down to these owners in more ways than one. The move was a practical decision; one of the owners has mobility problems that may advance, making accessible living—primarily on one floor—the best option. While giving up the multistory house, however, this family had no intention of giving up a home of distinction and beauty.

Architect Michael Kim made sure they didn't have to. In remodeling the 1954 house, he chose elegant materials, fine products, and exceptional design elements that spell luxury as well as comfort and convenience in a subtly nautical theme. Besides, the 5,000-square-foot (464.5 sq. m) house is characterized by large rooms and, as Kim points out, having ample space can be the biggest luxury of all.

By removing the old, U-shaped counter, Kim opened the kitchen to its full 21 1/2-foot (6.6 m) length. Kitchen designer Barbara Baratz helped him plan a new kitchen/breakfast area that is as easy to use as it is beautiful. The work center is in a corner, where the cook can use the oven, sink, trash/recycling cabinet, and island prep surface without having to move. Full-extension drawers in the crease of the corner are surprisingly deep, bringing a full complement of cooking accessories into reach. A cutting board nests in a drawer in the island, where it is convenient for a standing or seated user. The owners can sit at the kitchen desk to cut vegetables or use the computer. Smooth cork flooring is aesthetically pleasing and nonslip.

Crowning the kitchen is a handcrafted fir ceiling, reminiscent of a boat hull. Perimeter skylights under the raised ceiling and frosted glass interior transoms draw light into the room from an above-ceiling light well. Low-watt pendant fixtures are trained on the ceiling and work areas. The result of illumination from more than one direction is good general lighting with minimal shadows and clear task lighting.

A Tree House for all Ages

Kim produced a deluxe-size master bedroom by merging two bedrooms at the back of the house. For whimsy and easy outdoor access without steps, he created a private "tree house" off the bedroom—a screened porch perched a few feet above ground level and extending into the trees. Adjacent to the bedroom is an open-plan master bath. While the space provides a 5-foot (1.5 m) turning radius for a wheelchair, it also gives the owners a luxuriously large bathroom. For ease of movement and an unencumbered, open feel, just a slim partition—no door or compartment—separates the shower from the rest of the room. A gentle slope channels shower water to the drain in the nonskid tile floor.

The shower includes many universal design features—good lighting, a handheld shower spray, a shelf accessible from a seated position. The teak shower bench coordinates with the bathtub's elegant teak surround, which has extra space at each end and along the front for seating. The owners wanted teak not only for its beauty and nautical flavor but also for its warmth to the touch. (Sealed with tung oil, it needs to be reoiled once a year.)

The vanity is both accessible and luxurious, with a rich marble slab and integrated sink, sleek lever handles, and a complement of cabinetry at one side. It has rear-mounted pipes to allow legroom for a seated user, and the tiltable mirror above it can be adjusted for each person. Kim consulted the owner's physical therapist for specific advice on the best spots for grab bars around the room. He placed handsome grab bars at the tub and commode, and put blocking behind the walls elsewhere so that more can be installed later.

From the bathroom, the owners can go directly into the bedroom or into a large his-and-hers closet to dress for the day. Outfitted with adjustable height rods, shelves, and drawers, the closet is a move-through room, open to both bath and bedroom.

While the rooms in the original house were large, the hall and doorways were dark and narrow. Kim widened the hall, pierced its ceiling with a tubular skylight, and established 36-inch (.9 m)-wide doorways throughout, even installing wider panels to replace old pocket doors. All the doors, interior and exterior, have flush thresholds. Windows are easy-open casements, and like the doors, have lever handles.

The front door is above grade, but the steps have railings, and an extended copper overhang provides a gracious, weather-protected entry. At the back of the house, French doors open to a large mahogany deck with integrated ramp. Because the deck is nearly 16 feet (4.9 m) deep, it accommodates a ramp with a comfortable 1:12 incline. To avoid the front steps, the homeowner can enter the house here or through the garage, where a stair chair takes him to the first floor office level and on up to the spacious and beautiful heart of the home.

GREAT IDEA

Refrigerator Drawers

Refrigerator drawers are a natural solution for universal design kitchens because they make everything accessible—there's no straining to reach items that are too high, too low, or too far back in a tall, cavernous refrigerator. The refrigerator drawers in this kitchen have an added advantage: Placed at the end of the kitchen island, they can be reached from the kitchen table. While seated, the homeowners can pull open a drawer to grab a beverage or piece of fruit—it's like having a waiter standing by.

▲ Kim reoriented the kitchen to allow easy flow between the cooking and breakfast areas. Most storage in the kitchen is below the counter, and all cabinet and door handles—including those on the refrigerator drawers—are stylish, easily gripped bars. A ribbon of transoms brings in natural light; while pendant and undercabinet fixtures brighten the counter and work areas.

Flush-threshold exterior doors

Wide hallways

Generous lighting

Casement windows

Handheld shower spray

Large, doorless shower

Lever-style door, cabinet and faucet handles

Well-placed grab bars and blocking for more

Shower seat

Tiltable mirror over vanity

Bathtub surround with sitting/transfer space

Refrigerator drawers

Full-extension kitchen drawers

Easy-grip hardware

Large closet with adjustable components

Attractive exterior ramp

Before

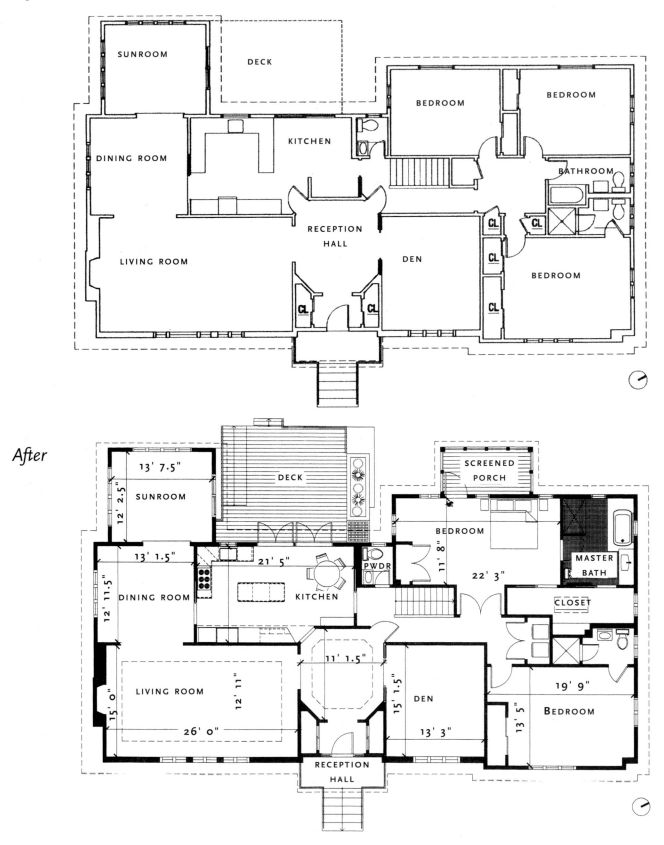

After

▲ With large, well-arranged rooms and broad openings between spaces, the floor plan didn't need a wholesale change. The architect made it more comfortable and accessible, though, by widening the doorways and hall, designing an open kitchen-eating area, converting two bedrooms and adjacent space into a large master suite, expanding the deck, and adding a screened porch.

▲ Flush-threshold French doors open to a mahogany deck with an elegant integrated ramp. The screened porch off the master bedroom is above ground but on the same level as the main floor.

▲ A standard product offering, these full-extension corner drawers bring utensils and cooking equipment into reach from both sides of the work corner.

▶ The teak bathtub surround is wide enough for seating on the side and ends; the faucets are easy to reach from inside or outside the bath; and the tub is undermounted so there is no raised edge to cross when getting in or out. Overhanging the tub surround, the sturdily attached marble vanity top can be grabbed for support.

INDEPENDENCE BY DESIGN

The owner of this house approaches life with gusto, and she wasn't about to let a house slow her down. At eighty-one years young, she rides horseback, keeps a garden full of vegetables and flowers, and frequently entertains family and friends. Healthy and energetic, she was living in a house that could have presented barriers down the road: It had steep, narrow stairs, no first-floor bedroom and bath, and no space for them. So architect Benjamin Nutter designed a new house for her—a small, low-maintenance place that suits her independent lifestyle and can easily be adapted for future needs.

The house has a second floor big enough for two bedrooms and a bath—an asset for resale—but everything the owner needs is on the first floor. Nutter left the second floor unfinished, simply insulating the space and roughing in the mechanicals so a caregiver apartment could be added cost effectively. The stairway runs from the entry foyer so that a caregiver could come and go without crossing into the owner's living space.

Spaces flow smoothly on the 1,742-square-foot (161.8 sq. m) first floor. The living and dining areas share a sunny open space. Low, tight-weave carpet and a wall of low-threshold sliding glass doors lead to the deck and horse pastures beyond. Another wide, low-threshold doorway opens to a screened porch, where the owner can enjoy the outdoors rain or shine. The lofty shed ceiling of the living area, rising from the patio doors to a peak in the center of the house, fills the room with natural light. Three tie beams over the living area define the space and make it more intimate, while recessed ceiling lights bathe the dining area in warm light. Although the kitchen is open to the living space, its flat ceiling, wood floor and suite of gray cabinetry give it a flavor of its own. An island defines the kitchen entry. Because the owner is barely 5 feet (1.5 m) tall, the island is tabletop height, 30 inches (76.2 cm), rather than the usual 36-inch (.9 m) counter height. It's a comfortable place for the owner to work standing, or to use as a casual dining table, with standard height chairs.

The sink is at the center of an efficient work corner, with a dishwasher on one side and a pullout trash bin within easy reach on the other. Most of the kitchen storage is below the counter, where it's easy to reach, and most is configured as drawers riding on full-extension, easy glide hardware. Open shelves by the refrigerator store pantry supplies, and a set of drawers and glass-fronted shelves recessed into an alcove form a built-in hutch that accessorizes the living area but absorbs no circulation space. A cabinet over the kitchen counter stores cookbooks and appliances; it's shallower than the counter, leaving landing space in front for appliances being brought out or put away. Easy-grip loop handles on all the drawers and cabinets are big enough for the owner to insert her whole hand. The faucet is a single lever, easy-to-control model. All the kitchen windows are crank-open casements, much easier to open over the counters than double-hung units.

A generous hall, or small room, joins the master bedroom and bath to the living space, enabling the bathroom to double as a guest bath. Wide doors open to the bedroom and bath. When the bedroom door is closed, the bookcase-lined hall serves as a warm anteroom leading to the bathroom.

A Closet for All Seasons

At more than 250 square feet (23.2 sq. m), the bedroom is large, and for good reason. The room has two walk-in closets, one for summer clothes and one for winter clothes, so the owner never has to lug out-of-season clothes to

◄ All the main living areas, interior and exterior, are on one level. Ceiling treatments, rather than confining walls, define the dining and living sections. Low, tight-weave carpeting and polyurethane-sealed pine flooring assure smooth footing.

storage. Thinking ahead, the owner wanted to be sure there was extra room for caregivers to move around in case she becomes bedridden. The bathroom contains a low vanity and sink; a large acrylic shower surround with overhead spray, handheld shower, grab bars and integrated acrylic bench; a handy linen closet; and ample circulation area.

Unlike most houses, where the ground floor is not really at ground level but as much as two feet above it, this house is very close to grade. Nutter achieved this by designing a shelf within the concrete foundation and dropping most of the wood floor framing down onto it. Two 6-inch (15.2 cm)-high steps lead to the front entry. The treads are 12 inches (30.5 cm) deep, to accommodate a person's whole foot. Constructing a ramp up the low rise would be simple, and the 6-by-12-foot (1.8 × 3.7 m) covered entry porch is big enough for someone in a walker or wheelchair to maneuver on. A glass-enclosed breezeway connects the garage to the house, providing cover from the weather without sacrificing light. There are several steps down to the garage and the cellar, wide enough to accommodate a stair chair.

While the homeowner loves to be outdoors, she would rather be gardening than cutting the grass. She got her wish with this house. Raised plant boxes, about 28 inches (71.1 cm) high, bring her vegetable and flower gardens to table height for tending without bending. Wood chips and gravel cover the grounds, eliminating the lawn-mowing chore. The house has a large roof overhang and drip beds so it needs no gutters, allowing the owner to cross gutter cleaning off the list of home maintenance worries. Routine housecleaning chores got easier, too, thanks to a central vacuum system. The owner can sweep dust and dirt to a toe kick area with a foot pedal; she steps on the pedal and away goes the debris.

Entry close to grade

Covered entry

Table-height kitchen island

Undercounter kitchen storage

Low-threshold shower enclosure with integrated bench

Handheld shower spray with long hose

Grab bars

Smooth flooring

Central vacuum and kick-space vacuum pans

Large closets

Low-threshold doors

Easy-glide drawer hardware

Accessible outlets and light switches

Easy-to-use exterior steps

Raised plant beds

Low-maintenance grounds

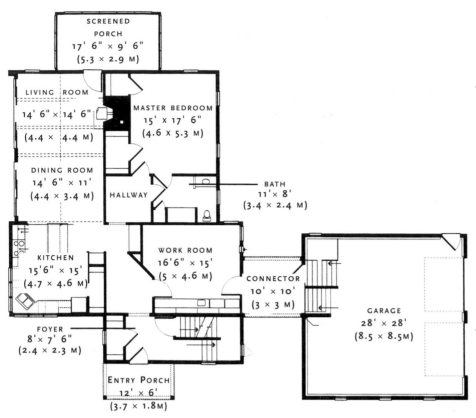

SCREENED
PORCH
17' 6" × 9' 6"
(5.3 × 2.9 M)

LIVING ROOM
14' 6" × 14' 6"
(4.4 × 4.4 M)

MASTER BEDROOM
15' × 17' 6"
(4.6 × 5.3 M)

DINING ROOM
14' 6" × 11'
(4.4 × 3.4 M)

HALLWAY

BATH
11' × 8'
(3.4 × 2.4 M)

KITCHEN
15'6" × 15'
(4.7 × 4.6 M)

WORK ROOM
16'6" × 15'
(5 × 4.6 M)

CONNECTOR
10' × 10'
(3 × 3 M)

GARAGE
28' × 28'
(8.5 × 8.5M)

FOYER
8' × 7' 6"
(2.4 × 2.3 M)

ENTRY PORCH
12' × 6'
(3.7 × 1.8M)

◄ Everything the owner needs for self-sufficient living is on the main floor of this cheery house, including an open indoor/outdoor entertaining area; a large master suite with wide-entry walk-in closets; and a multipurpose workroom linked to the garage by an enclosed breezeway. The unfinished second floor, which could become a caregiver apartment, has a private stairway in the foyer rather than in the owner's space.

▼ A table-height island marking the edge of the kitchen doubles as a food-prep aration station and breakfast table; outlets are conveniently located at each end. Handy built-in drawers and a display cabinet have the charm of a country hutch.

GREAT IDEA

Multipurpose Utility Room

Every universal design house needs a spacious laundry area, a home office, accessible storage space, and a hobby center—or at least a place to spread things out and wrap gifts or repot plants. In this house, all these functions are rolled into one good-size workroom where circulation space is shared. Adjacent to the garage, it has tabletops where the owner can put down bundles carried in from the car. The laundry center stretches across one wall of the room, and low, easily reached cubbies for gardening, cleaning, and hobby supplies line two other walls. A pet door and litter box occupy a corner by the door. Even with furnishings, there's plenty of space to move around in the multipurpose room. It's a room that offers the best of two worlds: It's convenient to use, and it concentrates a lot of messy functions in one place that can be hidden from visitors by closing the door.

◄ With raised plant boxes, the owner can garden without kneeling or squatting, and enjoy the blooms from her kitchen windows.

FAMILY-STYLE RANCH HOUSE

Ranch houses are a step ahead when it comes to universal design, since most of the living space is on one story. But that space often is tightly corralled. This 1950s ranch penned everything but the lower-level playroom and garage into a crowded 1,510-square-foot (140.3 sq. m) box. Architect David Pill took advantage of the large yard to open the design gates, adding three clever extensions that bring space, light and new versatility to the house.

Crafted for working parents and their two young children, the remodel incorporates a dynamic open family area, out-of-the-traffic-pattern workspace for the parents, and a private bedroom wing. Pill first removed the central stairway that split the living area into awkward compartments, replacing it with a jauntily angled stairwell on the side of the house. On the main floor, he designed a new master bedroom and bath suite, plus kids' rooms, all separated from the house's central core by a broad, sunny hall set at that same jaunty angle. A home-office addition occupies a quiet corner of the walkout basement. For ample outdoor access, Pill added a small deck off the kitchen and a bigger deck that wraps around the courtyard of the newly U-shaped, 3,860-square-foot (258.6 sq. m) house.

Because the house sits on a rise, both the garage level and main level are essentially on grade. An outdoor ramp from the garage to the main level could easily be added. When he expanded the reach of the house, Pill used posts to keep it level even where the ground slopes away. A broad section of the wraparound deck rests on posts so that the living space flows smoothly through French doors onto this outdoor seating area. The cantilevered kitchen deck has the added benefit of sheltering the lower-level, mudroom entry.

Pill expanded the kitchen into former bedroom space, creating one large living/dining/kitchen area that has neither narrow doorways nor confining walls. Two compact structures help define zones within the open plan without cutting into the circulation space. One contains closets. The other keeps many kitchen essentials—inset ovens, refrigerator, message center,

snack/coffee counter, and desk—within easy reach. Circulation space is generous in the heart of the kitchen as well as the pantry area, where double doors make every corner of the shelves accessible.

Windows of Opportunity

Pill reused the existing window openings around the house, enlarging them to bring in more light and match the oversize window and door openings on the additions. One practical exception—a small window over the kitchen counter—is used as a pass-through, reducing the need to carry things to and from the kitchen deck. Large windows lining the new stairwell wash the stairs and the adjacent living area with natural light. At the top of the stair wall, the light passes through built-in storage cubes with translucent plastic doors. The cubes themselves provide a gripping surface for stair users and low, easy-to-reach cabinetry.

Floor-to-ceiling windows in the children's bedrooms enable even tots to enjoy the sun and views. An ingenious mix of doors makes the master bedroom larger or smaller, private or open to the outdoors. Pocket doors at each end of the hall can be closed to enfold the hall into the bedroom itself. Sliding glass doors across from the bedroom open to the courtyard, and three large shoji screen sliding doors on flush tracks can be arranged in any way, from fully closing the bedroom to fully opening it. Even when the screens are closed, light from the courtyard filters through to brighten the bedroom.

◄ Large windows and sliding glass doors fill the stairway with light; translucent cabinet doors let the light pass through to the living space. The top of the stair wall, including the integrated cabinet, offer a place to hang on when climbing the stairs.

Wide-entry sliding doors

Level indoor/outdoor access

Doors to deck from several areas of house

Deep roof overhang for shade

Smooth flooring

Wide hallways

Rolling island in kitchen with heavy-duty, hospital-grade, lockable wheels

Easy-grip, rod-style handles

Bathroom and shower seating

Handheld shower spray

Pedestal sink

Translucent plastic cabinet doors

Ample windows and recessed can lights

Covered entry

Rather than a walk-in closet, the master bedroom has a walk-through closet that's equally accessible and that doubles as a passageway to the master bathroom. An unobtrusive pocket door can close off the bathroom. Pill designed a space-efficient, multipurpose structure for the master bath just as he did for the kitchen. Here, a bench and glass wall separate the bathroom entry from the shower. On one side of the glass, the bench works as seating for the bathroom or closets; on the other side it's a shower bench. The wide-entry shower could be made curbless or provided with a low, rollover curb.

For easy access, Pill placed the laundry room on the main floor of the house, conveniently located at the foot of the bedroom wing (where it can share plumbing conduits with the master bath). For quiet, he put the home office addition at one end of the basement. He made good lighting a priority, even in this back corner; a skylight sweeps across one side of the room, soaking in the sunlight.

The Island That Becomes a Peninsula

Sometimes, homeowners need a kitchen island, and other times, they want more counter space. This island offers both. Mounted on attractive, brightly colored, lockable wheels, it can be pulled wherever it's needed for use as a breakfast bar, buffet, work center, or play station. Shelves store kitchen supplies on one side and play supplies on the other; the overhanging countertop provides legroom for seated users. When more counter space is needed, the island links to the kitchen counter; the notched corner of the island top connects with the counter like a puzzle piece to form a seamless extension.

◄ A well-lighted, uncluttered space with a sweeping mirror, legroom under the sink, a large shower, bench seating, and a handheld shower, the master bath has many universal design features. Adding a few grab bars and a curbless shower entry would make it even more accessible.

◄ Lots of function is packed into the kitchen without sacrificing convenience or circulation space. Appliances, a desk, and a snack counter are tucked into one compact structure, and the island can be moved aside for open access to the kitchen.

▲ The house encloses a courtyard with a wrap-around, one-level deck that's accessible from kitchen, living area, and master bedroom. Deep roof overhangs provide shade.

Before

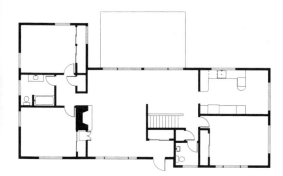

After

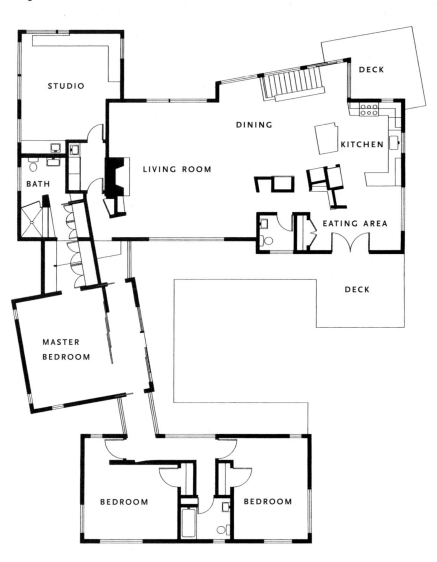

STUDIO

DINING

DECK

KITCHEN

BATH

LIVING ROOM

EATING AREA

DECK

MASTER
BEDROOM

BEDROOM

BEDROOM

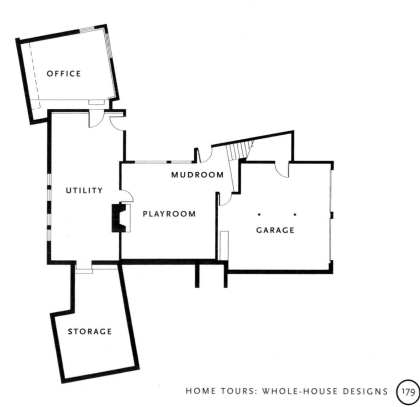

OFFICE

MUDROOM

UTILITY

PLAYROOM

GARAGE

STORAGE

▶ Before it was remodeled, this boxy ranch house was an awkward cluster of small rooms and narrow doorways. To update it for a young family, Pill applied many universal design principles: open, smooth-floored spaces; wide hallways; good natural and electric lighting; level indoor/outdoor connections; easy-access storage; and a large shower.

TOP-FLIGHT LIFESTYLE

One-floor living doesn't have to be ground-floor living. To enjoy the best river views, the empty-nesters who own this two-story, hillside house opted to live on the top floor. Despite space and budget limitations, architect Catherine Purple Cherry produced a house that lives large, celebrates the scenic setting, and is full of universal design comforts.

Getting to the top floor is as easy as pushing a button, thanks to a residential elevator. For those who want to climb, a staircase wraps around the elevator shaft. The custom elevator brings light and sparkle to the whole house. With glass on three sides, it doubles as a light tower, absorbing sunlight from adjacent windows and sharing it with living space on the first-floor guest room level and in the top-floor suite. The elevator also brings light to a third space, a lofty entryway on the same level as the driveway, but midway between the first floor and basement. The elevator cab is 6 inches (15.2 cm) longer and wider than the standard 3-by-4 feet (.9 × 1.2 m) to enable a wheelchair to turn and face the side exits into the living areas.

For smooth, safe access, the owners chose a front entry door that has no threshold.

The top floor is only 1,250 square feet (116.13 sq m), but the open space and sweep of windows overlooking the water make it seem larger. French doors with a flush threshold fold back against the wall, essentially merging the living area with the screen porch. Unless company is coming, the homeowners leave the extra-wide bedroom door open, too, enhancing the circulation flow and sense of space.

In the Zone

The living area is essentially one airy room organized into living, dining, and kitchen zones. One of the owners uses a cane and, after living for years in an old center-hall colonial house, he loves that everything is close by, not separated by winding halls and narrow doors. Just off the kitchen are the powder room and laundry. The house was cut into the hillside, making it possible for an exterior door to be located at the laundry room for quick exit from the top floor in case of emergency.

▼ The corner kitchen works well as both a food-prep center and an entertainment hub. There's seating space on two sides of the island for eating or working.

Designs for any house, but especially a universal design one, tend to evolve as products are discovered and patterns of use are considered. The laundry room exit door was one of many brainstorms that Lauer Construction, the builder, contributed along the way.

When planning the kitchen, the homeowners factored in their own operating styles as well as general ease of use. There's legroom on two sides of the island so the owners and their guests can sit to eat or prepare dinner. Since the owner who does most of the food preparation tends to move things from left to right, the sink in the island occupies a right-hand corner. And it faces the living-dining area so he can join in the conversation with guests while working in the kitchen.

Almost all of the appliances, from the side-by-side refrigerator/freezer to the warming drawer, can be used without a lot of bending or reaching. The stacked dishwasher drawers have enough capacity to handle a party; for day-to-day use, the owners stick to the more convenient top unit. A curtain conceals the stash of cleaning supplies under the sink. If a seated user needs to pull up to the sink, the space is ready.

The architect reserved a private quadrant of the suite for a luxurious master bathroom. Large enough for wheelchair maneuverability, it features a curbless shower, a tub with wide surround for seating, and a chair-height commode. Shallower joists under the shower allow its floor to slope slightly for drainage. Separate vanities work best for these homeowners; one is higher than standard so the husband doesn't have to bend. The other, designed like a dressing table for a seated user, is lower than standard. Good-looking grab bars—black nylon-coated models in the shower and metallic bars around the room that are designed to double as towel holders—provide style and support. Thinking ahead, the owners upgraded the side panels of the large vanity to plywood so that grab bars can be installed there if needed.

Adjacent to the bathroom is a walk-in master closet. The few hanging rods in the closet are low and easily reached, but not much is on them. Most of the owners' clothing, including shoes, is organized in convenient, adjustable drawers and shelves.

As of yet, these homeowners have no grandchildren. But when they do, the house is ready. Like the master bath, the first floor bathrooms have lever-handle faucets that are easy for small hands to turn.

GREAT IDEA

Barn Door

Want a wide door opening, but not at the price of a large swinging door or a pocket door that requires a track across the threshold? Install a barn door, which hangs from readily available ceiling-mounted hardware and rides on inset base rollers. This economical MDF (medium density fiberboard) door was custom made by the home builder. At 5 feet (1.5 m) across, it's as broad as a wall panel—and looks like one, with canvas murals framed by molding on each side.

▲ When the weather is nice, the homeowners open all the French doors and extend the living space onto the porch. The door openings are generous and there are no thresholds to get in the way.

▶ Enclosing the elevator in glass puts it in the limelight as a design feature and brings extra light into the house.

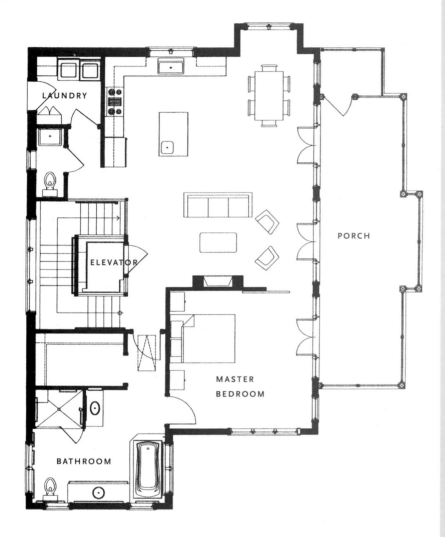

Covered, at-grade entry

Flat-threshold (ADA) doors

Casement windows

Lever door handles and faucets

Elevator

Side-by-side refrigerator/freezer

Dishwasher drawers

Warming drawer

Adjustable closet organizer system

Chair-height toilets

Grab bars

Curbless shower

Handheld shower spray

Tub surround with seating/ transfer space

Custom-height vanities

Nonskid tile bathroom floor

Smooth flooring in living space

Gas fireplace with accessible switch

▲ To capitalize on indoor/outdoor access, the top-floor living area features a broad porch accessible from both the great room and master bedroom. Bathrooms, elevator, stairs, and laundry line the back of the space. The suite is stacked over a three-bedroom, two-bath guest level and a basement with an exterior door a few steps below grade.

AGING GRACEFULLY

Like many people their age, the fifty-something owners of this 1963 ranch house had reached a transition point. They had octogenarian parents who found the house increasingly difficult to negotiate when they came to visit. One of the owners had begun working as a consultant and needed a home office. And, having made do for years with a small master bathroom and skimpy closets, the homeowners were ready to reward themselves with a larger, more comfortable master suite.

They faced three big questions. First, should they revamp their existing, 3,000-square-foot (278.7 sq. m) house or build a new house where lots were available farther from the center of town? They decided to stay in their current neighborhood, with its mature trees and convenient location. Second, should the remodeling plan focus only on short-term needs, or be more forward thinking? As long as they were going to invest in a major remodel, they opted for a design that would suit them in their retirement years—that is, a house where they could age in place. Finally, should they build a second story or enlarge the main level? They opted to expand the first floor, in part because the lot was large enough, and in part because they knew and liked one-floor living.

Approaching the remodel as an aging-in-place project, Doug Walter and associate Hamid Khellaf of Doug Walter Architects incorporated many subtle universal design features, and prepared the structure for the hassle-free addition of others later. As Walter puts it, the house is 90 percent accessible. It is 100 percent inviting.

Spacious Remodel

One of the most important, and most transparent, changes has to do with space and circulation. Walter rearranged interior walls to create an open flow of living spaces and extra-wide hallways. An entry foyer and library addition at the front of the house ties into the open plan, carrying views and circulation from front to back. Three other additions—the master suite extension, the home office, and a laundry room—bring the size of the remodeled house to a generous 4,200 square feet (390.2 sq. m).

Good lighting goes hand in hand with open space planning to make a house hospitable and safe. Walter achieved a rich mix of lighting in this house with recessed can lights, task lights, and a balance of natural light from windows, French doors and skylights. To pour natural light into the guest bathroom, he pierced the roof with a tubular skylight. Another tubular skylight brightens the basement staircase, which Walter rebuilt using an extra tread to produce a string of shallow, 6-inch (15.4 cm) risers with handrails on both sides. A clerestory window brings light from the dining room to an adjacent, windowless guest bedroom without sacrificing privacy.

Walter made the kitchen more accessible and friendly by eliminating the kitchen peninsula and designing a larger, more versatile island with inset cooktop. The change broadened the kitchen/great room connection, made it easier to get around in the kitchen, and created a comfortably sized working triangle between the oven/cooktop, sink, and refrigerator.

All doors throughout the house are low or no threshold and at least 3 feet wide (.9 m) wide for walker and wheelchair accessibility. At the doorway to the new master suite and to one guest bath, Walter used gracious, equally accessible double doors. French doors connect the dining room, library, and office to the outdoors; low-threshold sliding glass doors link the kitchen to the patio. For now, visitors can enter the house via the garage, kitchen, or dining room without encountering any steps. The 6-inch (15.4 cm) stoop at the front door will easily accommodate a ramp should the owners want one.

Suite Life

The master suite is all that the homeowners dreamed of. Each partner has a spacious, wide-entry walk-in closet with ample circulation space and a full complement of adjustable shelving. In the large, skylighted bathroom, the elegant his-and-hers vanities have matching cantilevered sinks, for beauty as well as wheelchair access, and are at different heights to suit each person. The owners chose a bathtub with integral handles that do the job of grab bars without fanfare. The shower has a built-in bench, a vertical grab bar to provide support by the entry, and two showerheads—one overhead and one adjustable, handheld model by the bench. A wedge could be inserted to ease entry across the shower threshold, but the shower is not big enough for a wheelchair. During construction, blocking was placed in the shower walls for additional grab bar installation. The accessible guest bath has handsome oiled bronze-finish grab bars that coordinate with the other fittings in the room, and a shower bench with its own handheld shower control in addition to the overhead spray.

Little things can go far to equip a house for the homeowners to age in place. Walter specified lever door handles throughout the house, and rocker light switches, including lighted ones for bathrooms. He installed motion sensor lights in closets and halls. The lights in the master closets are on timers so there is no stumbling around in the morning darkness.

The homeowners are delighted with their new dream house, and they are happy knowing that it will be able to adapt to their needs for many years to come.

▲ The living spaces open to each other, sharing a sweep of smooth, white oak flooring, light, and views. Ceiling treatments give each room definition. Perimeter uplighting reflects off the polished ceiling to provide general lighting throughout the great room.

Before

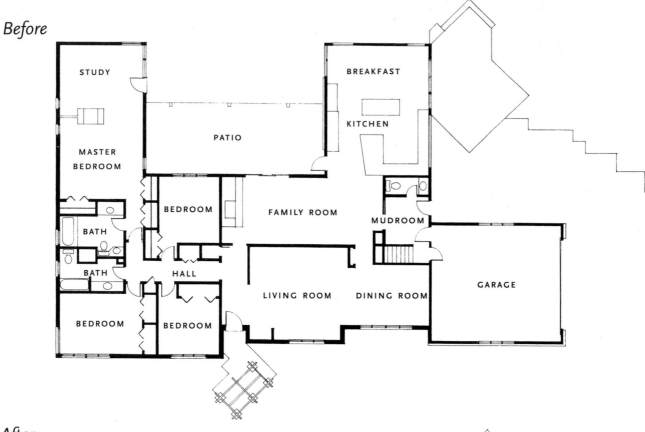

STUDY

BREAKFAST

KITCHEN

PATIO

MASTER BEDROOM

BEDROOM

FAMILY ROOM

MUDROOM

BATH

GARAGE

BATH

HALL

LIVING ROOM

DINING ROOM

BEDROOM

BEDROOM

After

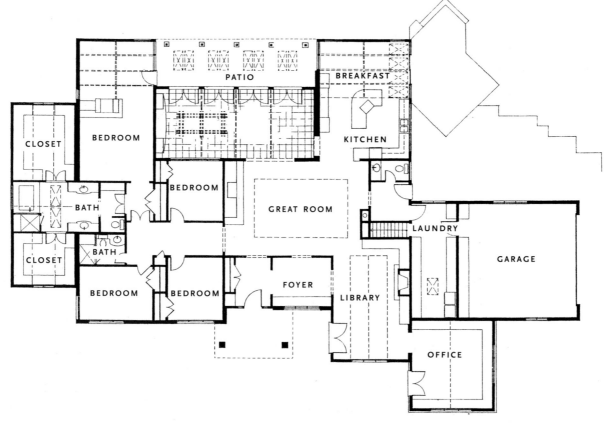

CLOSET

BEDROOM

BREAKFAST

PATIO

KITCHEN

BEDROOM

BATH

GREAT ROOM

CLOSET

LAUNDRY

BATH

GARAGE

BEDROOM

BEDROOM

FOYER

LIBRARY

OFFICE

▲ Walter pulled open the plan, moving interior walls to create an open living area, broad hallways, and doorways at least 3 feet wide (.9 m) wide. He filled out the house with additions on all four sides—an office, library, and new front entry; a dining room and patio; a laundry room; and an extension that includes an accessible guest bath and makes the master suite bigger and more user friendly.

No-step entries

Low- and no-threshold doors

Wide halls and doorways

Smooth flooring

Lever door handles

Generous lighting from windows, skylights, and fixtures

Rocker light switches

Shower benches

Fixed and handheld shower sprays

Custom-height vanities

Cantilevered sinks

Chair-height toilets

Tub with integral grab bars

Grab bars

▲ To facilitate circulation and use by two people, the bathing area is at one end of the master bath, the vanities at the other. Set at different heights for tall and shorter users, the vanities have accessible, over-hung sinks. A mix of skylights, windows, and fixtures fills the room with light. The matte-finish tile flooring is nonglare and slip-resistant.

UNIVERSAL DESIGN RESOURCES

GUIDELINES AND REGULATIONS

Accessible design regulations have been established at many levels of government, from federal to local. In the United States, the most widely applied model is the American National Standards Institute (ANSI) Accessible and Usable Buildings and Facilities A117.1, copyrighted by the International Code Council. Other major standards and resources include the Americans with Disabilities Act (ADA) Standards for Accessible Design (ADAAG), the Uniform Federal Accessibility Standards (UFAS), and the Fair Housing Accessibility Guidelines (FHAG).

While these standards are not required for most homes, they do provide practical guidelines. The following basic recommendations come from one or more of the published standards. (The full standards are considerably more extensive and detailed.)

By observing what works best for their clients, residential universal design practitioners have developed their own standards as well. These vary from designer to designer, but some are included here in [brackets].

Appliances
[Cooktop maximum 34 inches (86.4 cm) above floor]

[Dishwasher raised to align top rack with countertop]

[Refrigerator drawers occupying space starting 1 1/2 feet (45.7 cm) above floor]

Commode
[Seat 17 to 19 inches (43.2 to 48.3 cm) above floor, though standard height may be better for some people]

[18-to-36-inch (45.7 to 91.4 cm) clearance at front and side]

Countertops and work surfaces
Height: 28 to 34 inches (71.1 to 86.4 cm) [up to 42 inches (106.7 cm) for tall people]

Width: minimum 30 inches (76.2 cm)

Depth: maximum 27 inches (68.6 cm)

Knee clearance for seated users: 27 inches (68.6 cm) high, at least 17 inches (43.2 cm) deep, and at least 30 inches (76.2 cm) wide

Toe clearance under base cabinets: 9 inches (22.9 cm) high, at least 6 inches (15.2 cm) deep, at least 30 inches (76.2 cm) wide

Doorways
Width: clearance of at least 32 to 34 inches (81.3 to 86.4 cm) with door open ([a 34-inch [86.4 cm]-wide door provides a 32-inch [81.3 cm] clearance; a 36-inch [91.4 cm]-wide door provides a 34-inch [86.4 cm] clearance])

Threshold: .25-inch to .5-inch (6 mm to 1.3 cm) height; .75 inch (1.9 cm) for exterior sliding doors [Thresholds flush with the floor are best for all doors.]

Electrical outlets
Height: 15 inches (38.1 cm) above floor [18 to 25 inches (45.7 to 63.5 cm)]

Floor space, general
Minimum 5-foot (1.5 m)-diameter clear, turning space in every room and turning area [6 feet (1.8 m) is even better]

Grab bars
Width: 1.25 inch to 1.5 inch (3.1 to 3.8 cm) diameter
Clearance from wall: 1.5 inches (3.8 cm)

Hallways
Width: 36 inches (91.4 cm) [42 to 48 inches (106.7 to 121.9 cm), depending on location and use]

Hardware
36 to 48 inches (91.4 cm to 121.9 cm) above floor [36 inches (91.4 cm) is preferred]

Kitchen floor space
Pass-through kitchen with turning space at each end: minimum 40 inches wide (101.6 cm) [minimum 48 inches (121.9 cm) preferred]

U-shaped kitchen: minimum 60 inches (1.5 m) wide

Clear floor space at each workstation: minimum 30 by 48 inches (76.2 by 121.9 cm) [These spaces can overlap.]

Light switches, climate controls

General height: maximum 48 inches (121.9 cm) above floor [36 to 44 inches (91.4 to 111.8 cm) preferred]; a few inches lower if cabinet or counter limits access

Shower

[Minimum 3-by-3 feet (.9 by .9 m), though this does not allow room for a seat or for moving around; preferably 42 by 60 inches (106.7 by 1.5 m) or more]

Sinks

Height of front edge: maximum 34 inches (86.4 cm) [recommended range similar to that for countertops and work surfaces]

Depth to faucet: maximum 17 inches (43.2 cm) [12 inches (.3 m) preferred]

Clearance underneath: minimum 27 inches (68.6 cm) high [preferably 29 inches (73.7 cm)], 30 inches (76.2 cm) wide; maximum 17 inches (43.2 cm) deep, including 8 inches (20.3 cm) to under-sink pipes

Sink depth: maximum 6 ½ inches (16.5 cm)

Storage

Shelf height for accessibility by seated user: maximum 40 to 48 inches (101.6 to 121.9 cm)

Washer and dryer

Front loading, with door opening between 15 and 34 inches (38.1 to 86.4 cm) above floor [*Recommended minimum circulation space in front of machines:* 30 by 48 inches (76.2 by 121.9 cm)]

Windows

Maximum sill height for access and views: 36 inches (91.4 cm)

CODES AND STANDARDS

United States

ANSI Standard A117.1

American National Standards Institute (ANSI)

International Code Council

800.786.4452

www.iccsafe.org

Americans with Disabilities Act Standards for Accessible Design (ADAAG)

U.S. Department of Justice

800.514.0301

www.usdoj.gov/crt/ada/stdspdf.htm

U.S. Access Board

(Similar to ADA Accessibility Guidelines)

800.872.2253

www.access-board.gov/adaag/html/adaag.htm

Fair Housing Accessibility Guidelines (FHAG)

U.S. Department of Housing and Urban Development

800.767.7468

www.hud.gov/offices/fheo/disabilities/fhefhag.cfm

Uniform Federal Accessibility Standards (UFAS)

U.S. Access Board

800.872.2253

www.access-board.gov/ufas/ufas-html/ufas.htm

International

AS1428.1-2001 and AS1428.2-1992

AS4299-1995 Adaptable Housing Standard

Standards Australia International

02.9237.6000

www.standards.org.au

BS8300: 2001

British Standards Institution

44.20.8996.9001

www.bsi-global.com

CAN/CSA B651-04

Canadian Standards Association

800.463.6727

www.csa.ca

NZ Standard 4121:2001

Standards New Zealand

64 4 498 5994

www.standards.co.nz

International Best Practices in Universal Design: A Global Review

A 2006 publication by the Canadian Human Rights Commission that compares accessibility codes and standards from more than a dozen countries.

Canadian Human Rights Commission

888.214.1090

www.chrc-ccdp.ca

SPECIALISTS

Certified Aging-in-Place Specialist program (CAPS)

This aging-in-place/universal design training and designation program was developed by the National Association of Home Builders (NAHB) Remodelers in collaboration with the NAHB 50+ Housing Council, the NAHB Research Center (NAHBRC), and AARP. Enter CAPS in the search line at NAHB.org to find more information. There are hundreds of CAPS designees, including remodelers, builders, designers, accessibility experts, consultants, suppliers, occupational therapists, and others. The NAHB website includes a CAPS directory organized by location and business type. For the directory, go to www.nahb.org/directory.aspx?directoryID=188

Easy Access to Health

Universal design consulting and research business
1331 Green Mountain Drive
Livermore, CO 80536 USA
970.219.0212
www.agingbeautifully.org

Shared Solutions America

A national nonprofit organization that fosters universal design and accessible design of homes. The website lists several home building professionals that specialize in universal design.
974 Bremen Way
Alpine, CA 91901 USA
619.445.6778
www.livablehomes.org

Transgenerational Design Matters

A nonprofit research and education organization that assists with the design of products and environments for all ages and abilities
2007 Quail Run Drive, NE
Albuquerque, NM 87122 USA
505.821.9221
www.transgenerational.org

Universal Designed Smart Homes

Universal design house plans, information, and links
PO Box 533
Moline, IL 61266 USA
309.792.4599
www.universaldesignonline.com

Universal Designers & Consultants, Inc.

A business that provides design services, consulting, publications, and links to additional universal design resources
6 Grant Avenue
Takoma Park, MD 20912
301.270.2470
www.universaldesign.com

INFORMATION RESOURCES

AARP

This large national association features universal design and aging-in-place information, planning tools, and resources on its website.

601 E Street NW
Washington, DC 20049 USA
888.687.2277
www.aarp.org/families/home_design/

American Institute of Architects

Information on design for an aging population is on the organization's website; search for design for aging.

The American Institute of Architects
1735 New York Ave., NW
Washington, DC 20006 USA
800.AIA.3837 or 202.626.7300
www.aia.org

American Society of Interior Designers (ASID)

The national organization has an Aging-in-Place Council to inform its membership; the website provides general information on universal design, accessibility, and aging in place, including links for additional information and resources.

608 Massachusetts Ave., NE
Washington, DC 20002 USA
202.546.3480
www.asid.org
www.asid.org/knowledge/Universal+Design.htm

Australian Network of Universal Housing Design

Supporting universal design of homes in Australia, this organization offers publications and links to other resources

PO Box 666
Strawberry Hills NSW 2012, Australia
02.9370.3100
www.anuhd.org

Canadian Abilities Foundation

A central source of information on accessibility in Canada, including a section on housing.
340 College Street, Suite 401
Toronto, ON M5T 3A9
416.923.1885
http://abilities.ca/housing.html?show-housing=1

Center for Accessible Environments

Fosters accessibility of the built environment in the United Kingdom.

70 South Lambeth Road
London SW8 1RL England
020.7840.01
www.cae.org.uk

Center for Inclusive Design & Environmental Access (IDEA)

An information center that features universal design and product ideas.

378 Hayes Hall, School of Architecture & Planning
3435 Main Street
University of Buffalo
Buffalo, NY 14214 USA
716.829.3485, ext. 329
www.ap.buffalo.edu/idea/

Center for Universal Design

A dedicated source of information, technical assistance, guidelines, and publications on universal design.

North Carolina State University
School of Design
Box 8613
Raleigh, NC 27695 USA
919.515.3082
www.centerforuniversaldesign.org

Concrete Change

Advances a worldwide effort to design homes and facilities that meet visitability standards for people with disabilities.

600 Dancing Fox Road
Decatur, GA 30032 USA
404.378.7455
www.concretechange.org

European Concept for Accessibility

Provides information about accessible housing and other facilities, offers publications, and lists links to other sites and organizations in Europe and the United States.
www.eca.lu

European Institute for Design and Disability

Functions as a communications center on accessible design throughout Europe.

via Sumpiazzo 9
23865 Oliveto Lario (LC) Italy
39.031.968025
www.design-for-all.org

Satoshi Kosi

Professor Kosi posts Japanese universal design guidelines and related links on his website.

Department of Architecture, Faculty of Design, Shizuoka University of Art and Culture
2-1-1 Chuo, Hamamatsu 430-8533 Japan
81.53.457.6225
http://homepage2.nifty.com/skose/

National Aging in Place Council (NAIPC)

Promotes aging-in-place through information on residential design and home financing

1400 16th St. NW, Suite 420
Washington, DC 20036 USA
202.939..1784
www.naipc.org

National Association of Home Builders

The consumer section of this industry association website provides information on universal design and aging in place. For information on builders and remodelers who specialize in the field, enter 50 Plus Housing Council and NAHB Remodelers in the search line. For technical guidelines, enter NAHB Research Center in the search line. See below for more on the research center.

1201 15th Street, NW
Washington, DC 20005
202.266.8200, ext.0
800.368.5242
www.nahb.org

NAHB Research Center, Inc. (NAHBRC)

A subsidiary of NAHB, the research center provides universal design technical guidelines, extensive product and manufacturer list, links to other resources through www.ToolBase.org. The Center produces an annual guide to accessible products, which can be viewed on the website (www.ToolBase.org/dabp) or purchased.

400 Prince George's Boulevard
Upper Marlboro, MD 20774 USA
800.638.8556

National Association of the Remodeling Industry (NARI)

In spring 2008, this industry association launched a professional remodeler education and certification program in universal remodeling. The NARI website lists remodelers by specialty and location.

780 Lee St, Suite 200
Des Plaines, IL 60016 USA
800.611.6274
www.nari.org

National Kitchen and Bath Association

The website of this association of professional kitchen and bath designers includes a section for consumers, with information on planning safe kitchens and baths.
800.843.6522
www.nkba.org

National Resource Center on Supportive Housing and Home Modification

Andrus Gerontology Center, University of Southern California
The center serves as a clearinghouse of information on accessible design and products.

3715 McClintock Avenue
Los Angeles, CA 90089 USA
213.740.1364
www.homemods.org

Smart Housing

The Queensland, Australia, government smart housing section is devoted to housing that has universal design features and is socially, environmentally, and economically sustainable. The website includes guidelines and links.

Queensland Government Works Division
Department of Public Works
Level 6A, 80 George Street,
GPO Box 2457
Brisbane Qld 4001 Australia
07.3227.7451
www.smarthousing.qld.gov.au

Universal Design Living Laboratory

A model accessible home and universal design information source

1008 Eastchester Drive
Columbus, OH 43230
614.471.6100
www.udll.com

World of Universal Design

Identifying universal design information and design resources around the world, this site is a section of the Center for Inclusive Design & Environmental Access (IDEA), listed above.
www.ap.buffalo.edu/idea/wud/Info.htm

MANUFACTURERS

★ More and more manufacturers are offering attractive and practical products appropriate for universal design. The following list identifies some of them. Most have some international distribution; those marked with an asterisk sell products only in the United States at this time, but companies in other countries offer similar products.

Appliances

Asko
www.asko

Fisher & Paykel Appliances
www.fisherpaykel.com

Gaggenau
www.gaggenau.com

GE
www.ge.com

Marvel Industries
www.lifeluxurymarvel.com

Miele
www.miele.com

Sharp
www.sharp-world.com

Sub-Zero
www.subzero.com

U-Line
www.u-line.com

Whirlpool
www.whirlpool.com

Bathroom and kitchen

★ **AD-AS**
www.ad-as.com

American Standard
www.americanstandard.com

Kohler
www.kohler.com

Moen
www.moen.com

Bathroom fixtures, fittings, grab bars, and accessories

★ **Alsons Corporation**
www.alsons.com

★ **Aqua Bath**
www.aquabath.com

★ **BathEase**
www.bathease.com

★ **Best Bath Systems**
www.best-bath.com

★ **C. D. Sparling**
www.cdsparling.com

★ **Clarion Bathware**
www.clarionbathware.com

★ **Comfort Designs**
www.comfortdesignsbathware.com

E. L. Mustee & Sons
www.mustee.com

Elcoma
www.elcoma.com

Estoli
www.estoli.com

Franklin Brass
www.franklinbrass.com

Gerberit
www.geberit.com

★ **Ginger**
www.gingerco.com

Great Grabz
www.greatgrabz.com

Great Grips
www.greatgrips.com

★ **HEWI**
www.hewi.com

★ **Jaclo Industries**
www.jaclo.com

Lasco
www.lascobathware.com

MAAX
www.maax.com

Oceania Baths
www.oceaniabaths.com

★ **Porcher**
www.porcher-us.com

★ **Robern**
www.robern.com

★ **Speakman**
www.speakmancompany.com

Wingits.com
www.wingits.com

Cabinets, storage, and storage accessories

* **Automated Cabinet Systems**
   www.automatedcabinetsystems.com

   Blum
   www.Blum.com

   California Closets
   www.californiaclosets.com

   Crown Point Cabinetry
   www.crown-point.com

   ClosetMaid
   www.closetmaid.com

* **Diamond Cabinets**
   www.diamondcabinets.com

   Hafele
   www.hafele.com

   Kraftmaid
   www.kraftmaid.com

   LEMA
   www.lemamobili.com

* **Marsh Furniture Company**
   www.marshfurniture.com

   Neff
   www.neffkitchens.com

   Rev-a-Shelf
   www.revashelf.com

* **Roll-out Shelf Co.**
   www.rolloutshelf.com

* **Shelf Conversions**
   www.shelfconversions.com

* **Wellborn Cabinets**
   www.wellborn.com

Doors, Windows, Window Coverings

Andersen Windows and Doors
www.andersenwindows.com

Hunter Douglas
www.hunterdouglas.com

LUALDI
www.lualdi.com

Marvin Windows and Doors
www.marvin.com

ODL
www.odl.com

Therma-Tru
www.thermatru.com

Velux
www.velux.com

* **Great Grips (doorknob converter)**
   www.greatgrips.com

Residential elevators

* **Concord Elevator & Lift**
   www.conccordelevator.com

* **National Wheelovator**
   www.wheelovator.com

* **Thyssenkrupp Access**
   www.tkaccess.com

* **Waupaca Elevator Company**
   www.waupacaelevator.com

Specialty

BEGA (exterior lighting)
www.bega.com

**Better Lifestyle Products
(fold-away ironing board)**
www.betterlifestyleproducts.com

* **Great Grabz (grab bars)**
   www.greatgrabz.com

   ODL (motorized window blinds)
   www.odl.com

   Velux (skylights, motorized window blinds)
   www.velux.com

* **Iron-A-Way (foldaway ironing board)**
   www.ironaway.com

* **Lindustries (Leveron doorknob converter)**
   781-237-8177

   Leviton (electrical switches)
   www.leviton.com

   **No Skidding Products Inc.
   (nonskid floor coating)**
   www.noskidding.com

   LUALDI (semitranslucent doors)
   www.lualdi.com

DESIGNER DIRECTORY

Abbie Joan Enterprises
4535 Domestic Avenue, Suite D
Naples, FL 34104
239-435-0677
www.abbiejoan.com

Alward Construction Company
780 San Luis Road
Berkeley, CA 94707
510-527-6498
www.alwardconstruction.com

Bentley Design & Remodeling
610 West 7th Street
Hanford, CA 93230
559-582-5561
www.bentleydesign.com

Brennan + Company Architects
640 Frederick Road
Baltimore, MD 21228
410-788-2289
www.brennanarch.com

Brenner Builders
362 Adams Street
Bedford Hills, NY 10507
914-242-4707
www.brennerbuilders.com

Thomas Buckborough & Associates
358 Great Road
Acton, MA 01720
978-263-3850
www.tbadesigns.com

CG&S Design-Build
402 Corral Lane
Austin, TX 78745
512-444-1580
www.cgsdb.com

Chandler Design Build
3249 Henderson Field Road
Mebane, NC 27302
919-304-5397
www.chandlerdesignbuild.com

Catherine Purple Cherry Architects, PC
1 Melvin Avenue
Annapolis, MD 21401
410-990-1700
www.purplecherry.com

Design Collaboratives, Inc.
3654 West Diversey Avenue
Chicago, IL 60647
773-227-3244
www.designcollaboratives.com

designworker
78 Conz Street
Northampton, MA 01060
413-538-0952
www.designworker.net

Devereaux & Associates
1481 Chain Bridge Road #302
McLean, VA 22101
703-893-0102
www.devereauxarch.com

Erickson Zebroski Design Group, Inc.
1246 18th Street
San Francisco, CA 94107
415-487-8660
www.ezdg.net

Mary Fisher Designs, Scottsdale, Arizona
PO Box 14393
Scottsdale, AZ 85267
480-473-0986
www.maryfisherdesigns.com

Andre G. Fontaine Architect
P.O. Box 357
Glenelg, MD 21737
410-531-3925

Ira Frazin, Architect
236 West. 26th Street #1103
New York, NY 10001
646-382-9963
www.ifarchitect.com

Full Circle Architects
1510 Old Deerfield Road, Suite 201
Highland Park, IL 60035
847-831-0084
www.fullcirclearchitects.com

Geiger Architecture
613 Main Street, #201
Rapid City, SD 57701
605-348-6062
www.geigerarchitecture.com

Great Kitchens, Inc.
3130 E. Madison Street
Seattle, WA 98112
206-324-6604
www.greatkitchensinc.com

Harrell Remodeling, Inc.
1954 Old Middlefield Way
Mountain View, CA 94043
650-230-2900
www.harrell-remodeling.com

Howell Design & Build, Inc.
360 Merrimack Street, Building 5
Lawrence, MA 01843
978-989-9440
www.howelldesignbuild.com

International Kitchens
13500 Bel-Red Road
Bellevue, WA 98005
425-274-7830
www.ikcooks.com

Johnson & Hodson Interior Design
161 East Broadway
Salt Lake City, UT 84111
801-575-6016
http://johnsonandhodson.com

Marsha Jones Interior Design Ltd.
324 South Hale Street
Wheaton, IL 60187
630-665-4615
www.marshajones.com

Michael Kim Associates
1 Holden Street #3
Brookline, MA 02445
617-739-6925
www.mkimarchitecture.com

Kitchen Encounters
202 Legion Avenue
Annapolis, MD 21401
410-263-4900
www.kitchenencounters.biz

Carol R. Knott, ASID, Interior Design
430 Green Bay Road
Kenilworth, IL 60043
847-256-6676

Kuche + Cucina Kitchens and Fine Interiors
489 Route 17
South Paramus, NJ 07652
201-261-5221
www.kuche-cuchina.com

Jane Langmuir, AIA
107 Bowen Street
Providence, RI 02906
407-274-5216

Legacy General contracting, Inc.
1185 W. Utah Avenue, Suite 102
PO Box 840709
Hildale, UT 84784
866-212-2443
www.legacygeneral.com

MWR Company
45431 South East Edgewick Road
North Bend, WA 98045
206-782-9491
www.mwrcompany.com

Mark IV Builders, Inc.
5161 River Road
Bethesda, MD 20816
240-395-9400
www.markivbuilders.com

T. McIntyre Associates
Penn Field
3601 South Congress Avenue
Building B, Suite 400A
Austin, TX 78704
512-712-9900
www.tmcintyre.com

McMonigal Architects, LLC
1224 Marshall Street NE, Suite 400
Minneapolis, MN 55413
612-331-1244
www.mcmonigal.com

Melville Thomas Architects, Inc.
600 Wyndhurst Avenue, Suite 245
Baltimore, MD 21210
410-433-4400
www.mtarx.com

Nash Jones Anderson Associates
Architects & Planners
11644 NE 80th St., #104
Kirkland, WA 98033
425- 828-4117
www.nashjonesanderson.com

Native Landscape Design and Restoration
PO Box 76
Free Union, VA 22940
434-975-2859

Norsk Remodeling
16725 Cleveland Street
Redmond, WA 98052
425-881-3539
www.norskhome.com

Neil Kelly Company
804 N. Alberta Street
Portland, OR 97217
503-288-7461
www.neilkell.com

Benjamin Nutter Architects
363 Boston Street
Topsfield, MA 01963
978-887-9836
www.benjaminnutter.com

Olsen Homes & Renovation
1339 Madison Street, NE
Salem, OR 97301
503-393-5067
www.olsenrenovation.com

One Earth One Design
14300 Greenwood Avenue N, Suite A
Seattle, WA 98133
206-418-8120
www.1earth1design.com

Otogawa-Anschel Design Build
1214 42nd Avenue North
Minneapolis, MN 55412
612-789-7070
www.otogawa-anschel.com

Mary Jo Peterson, Inc.
3 Sunset Cove Road
Brookfield, CT 06804 USA
203-775-4763
www.mjpdesign.com

Pill-Maharam Architects
5597 Shelburne Road
Shelburne, VT 05482
802-735-1286
www.pillmaharam.com

Post & Beam Design Build
112 Colvard Court
Forest Hill, MD 21050
410-515-6464
www.pbdesignbuild.com

Linda Randolph, AIA
37077 Bodily Avenue
Fremont, CA 94536
510-745-9318

Renovation Design Group, LLC
252 South 1300 East
Salt Lake City, UT 84102
801-533-5331
www.renovationdesigngroup.com

Catherine Roha, AIA
1705 Parker Street
Berkeley, CA 94703
510-845-1833

SawHorse, Inc.
2030 Powers Ferry Road, Suite 350
Atlanta, GA 30339
404-256-2567
www.sawhorse.net

Christopher Saxman Architect
851 Southeast Pioneer Way, #202
Oak Harbor, WA 98277
360-675-4414
http://saxmanarchitects.com

Schade & Bolender Architects
2118 Locust Street
Philadelphia, PA 19103
215-731-0390
www.schadeandbolender.com

Shirey Contracting, Inc.
230 NE Juniper Street
Issaquah, WA 98027
425-427-1300
www.shireycontracting.com

Showplace Design and Remodeling
8710 Willows Road, NE
Redmond, WA 98052
425-885-1595
www.showplaceinc.com

Studio Pacifica, Ltd.
2144 Westlake Avenue N, Suite F
Seattle, WA, 98109
206-292-9799
www.studiopacifica.com

Stylander Design Group
Wall Street Plaza
88 Pine Street, 11th floor
New York, NY 10005
212-269-3902
www.stylander.com

Sunrise Cedar Homes & Sunrooms
11403 58th Avenue E
Puyallup, WA 98373
877-327-1181

Tandem Design Group
1225 East Sunset Drive, #776
Bellingham, WA 98226
360-714-0879

David Tonnesen
1 Fitchburg Street, Loft #C113
Somerville, MA 02143
www.dtonnesen.com

Trivers Associates
100 North Broadway, Suite 1800
St. Louis, MI 63102
314-241-2900
www.trivers.com

Bonnie Ulin Inc.
892 Worcester Street
Wellesley, MA 02482-3718
781-235-1540
www.bonnieulininc.com

Village Carefree Communities
1265 East Fort Union Boulevard, Suite 100
Midvale, UT 84047
801-561-1000
www.village-communities.com

Doug Walter Architects
280 Columbine Street, Suite 205
Denver, CO 80206
303-320-6916
dw3206916@aol.com

White Rabbit Garage Organizers
3192 Doolittle Drive
Northbrook, IL 60062
847-272-7878
www.whiterabbitinc.com

Randall Whitehead Lighting, Inc.
1246 18th Street
San Francisco, CA 94107
415-626-1277
www.randallwhitehead.com

Gary Wolf Architects, Inc.
7 Marshall Street
Boston, MA 02108
617-742-7557
www.wolfarchitects.com

The Workshops of David T. Smith
3600 Shawhan Road
Morrow, OH 45152
888-353-9387
www.davidtsmith.com

Michael Wolk Design Associates
31 Northeast 28 Street
Miami, FL 33137
305-576-2898
www.wolkdesign.com

ACKNOWLEDGMENTS

Designers are pouring great creativity into universal design, and most seem as eager as I am to spread the word about this important and burgeoning field. My thanks to the many architects, designers, remodelers, builders, manufacturers, and specialists who so generously allowed me to share their fine ideas in this book.

I am grateful to Vince Butler, one of the first people to open my eyes to the promise and possibilities of beautiful universal design, and to the National Association of Home Builders Certified Aging-in-Place Specialist program (CAPS), for giving me the knowledge base from which to launch this book project. Special thanks go to Patricia Nunan, Mary Jo Peterson, John Salmen, and Louis Tenenbaum, who contributed their expertise along the way.

Quarry editors Laura Smith and Betsy Gammons are the cream of the crop; because of their good judgment, high standards, efficiency, and composure, working on the book was always a pleasure. Finally, I want to thank publisher Winnie Prentiss, who recognized instantly that this is a book that needed to be written.

ABOUT THE AUTHOR

An award-winning writer and editor with expertise in residential design and remodeling, Wendy A. Jordan is a certified aging-in-place specialist (CAPS). Author of numerous books on residential design and remodeling, she covers the industry for *Professional Remodeler* magazine, HGTVPro.com, and other magazines and websites. Before launching her own company, she was editor in chief of *Remodeling* magazine.

PHOTOGRAPHER CREDITS

Russell Abraham Photography/Alward Construction Co., 115 (top); 117

Russell Abraham Photography/Catherine Roha, AIA, 115 (bottom)

Courtesy of AD-AS, 73 (top, right)

Sandy Agrafiotis/Benjamin Nutter Architects, 27 (top); 170; 172 (bottom); 173

Courtesy of Alward Construction co., 116

Courtesy of American Standard/Porcher, 106 (bottom, left & right); 107 (top, right & left)

Dennis Anderson/Erickson Zebroski Design Group, Inc./Randall Whitehead Lighting, Inc., 79 (bottom); 111; 113

Courtesy of ASKO, 75 (bottom)

Courtesy of Automated Cabinet Systems, 36 (top, left)

Courtesy of BEGA, 37 (bottom)

Courtesy of Bentley Design & Remodeling, 58

Courtesy of Best Bath Systems, 104 (top, left)

Courtesy of Better Lifestyle Products, 34 (top, right); 109 (top, left)

Courtesy of Blum, 68 (bottom, left & right)

Brynn Bruijn/Abbie Joan Enterprises, 91; 92

Hunter Breedlove/Heidi Lawrence, AKBD/Neil Kelly Company, 6 (right); 60; 61

Thomas Buckborough & Associates, 86; 131

Courtesy of California Closets, 32 (top, right)

Catherine Purple Cherry Architects, P.C., 180; 181; 182; 183

Courtesy of ClosetMaid, 33 (bottom, left)

Courtesy of Concrete Change, 138

Devereaux & Associates P.C., 154; 155

Courtesy of Diamond Cabinets, 64

Carlos Domenech/Michael Wolk Design Associates, 78

Phillip Ennis Photography/Brenner Builders, 132 (top)

Phillip Ennis Photography/Kuche + Cucina Kitchens and Fine Interiors, 41

Bill Enos, Emerald Light Photography/Harrell Remodeling, 88; 89

Bill Enos, Emerald Light Photography/Olsen Homes & Renovation, 65 (top)

Courtesy of Estoli, 105 (top, right & bottom, left)

Courtesy Fisher & Paykel, 68 (top, left); 69 (bottom, right)

Rodolphe Foucher/Transgenerational Design Matters, 143; 144; 148; 149

Courtesy of Gaggenau, 74 (top, left & right); 75 (top, right)

Courtesy of GE Appliances, 67 (top); 74 (bottom, left)

Courtesy of GE Appliances/Mary Jo Peterson, Inc., 9 (top); 39; 46; 47; 48; 70 (top, left)

Courtesy of Ginger, 104 (bottom, right)

Alan Goldstein/Centex Homes/Devereaux & Associates P.C., 150; 152; 153; 157

Sam Gray/Michael Kim Associates, 165; 167; 168

Mike Gullon, Phoenix Photographic Studio/CKD, Kitchen Encounters, 67 (bottom)

Courtesy of Kohler Company, 79 (top); 84; 85; 108 (top, left); 109 (right & bottom, left)

Courtesy of Great Grabz, 104 (top, right); 105 (top, left)

Courtesy of Great Grips, 32 (top, left)

Chris Green/UniversalDesign.com, 42; 44; 45

Anne Gummerson/Brennan + Company Architects, 22 (bottom); 112

Anne Gummerson/Andre G. Fontaine, Architect, 6 (left); 26 (top); 101 (top);

Anne Gummerson Photography/Melville Thomas Architects, 101 (bottom, right); 119 (top & bottom)

Anne Gummerson/Post & Beam Design-Build, 100 (right)

Greg Hadley/Mark IV Builders, Inc., 23 (top); 30 (top); 132 (bottom)

Courtesy of Hafele, 68 (top, right); 69 (top, left); 71 (right); 72 (top, right); 105 (bottom, right); 106 (top, right)

Roger Hardy/Harrell Remodeling, 93 (bottom, right)

William Helsel/Bentley Design & Remodeling, 57; 59

Greg Hursley/Through the Lens Management/ CG&S Design-Build, 12; 140; 141

Michael Kim Associates, 166

Courtesy of KitchenAid and Whirlpool, 70 (bottom, right); 71 (top, left)

Courtesy of MAXX, 107 (bottom, right)

Courtesy of KraftMaid Cabinetry, 71 (middle, left & bottom); 72 (top, left)

Courtesy of Lasco Bathware, 109 (top, left)

Bob Lavellee/Thomas Buckborough & Associates, 7 (middle); 9 (bottom); 87; 97 (bottom); 129; 130; 131

Bjorg Magnea/Ira Frazin, Architect, 127

Bjorg Magnea/Stylander Design Group, 28 (bottom)

Courtesy of Manley Architecture Group/MAG, 17

Thomas McConnell/CG&S Design-Build/Through the Lens Management, 30 (bottom); 122; 124; 125

Thomas McConnell/Through the Lens Management/T. McIntyre Associates, Inc., 137 (top)

Courtesy of McCormack Baron Salazar/Trivers Associates, 161; 163

Courtesy of Melville Thomas Architects, Inc., 119

Courtesy of Moen, 36 (bottom, left); 108 (top & bottom, right); 109 (top, right)

INDEX